LET'S MOVE THE NEEDLE

AN ACTIVISM HANDBOOK
for Artists, Crafters,
Creatives, and Makers

SHANNON
DOWNEY
AKA Badass
Cross Stitch

The mission of Storey Publishing is to serve our customers by
publishing practical information that encourages
personal independence in harmony with the environment.

Edited by Diana Rupp and Sarah Guare Slattery
Art direction and book design by Alethea Morrison
Text production by Jennifer Jepson Smith

Cover and interior photography by Mars Vilaubi © Storey Publishing
Additional photography by © Aclosund Historic/Alamy Stock Photo, 26; Akilah Townsend, 31; Alex Yijia Ding, 205–206; © The American Society for the Prevention of Cruelty to Animals, 172; Aneesh Sankarankutty, 173 b.; APA, 173 t.; © Azoor Photo/Alamy Stock Photo, 22; © Guerrilla Girls, courtesy guerrillagirls.com, photo by Teri Slotkin, 27; Jayna Zweiman, 37; © Justin Hoffman/Greenpeace, 174; © Kevork Djansezian/Getty Images, 28; © Kues/Shutterstock.com, 44 white spray paint, 96 blue spray paint, 111 yellow spray paint, 148 yellow spray paint; Library of Congress, Prints & Photographs Division, American National Red Cross Collection, LC-DIG-anrc-06039, 24; Courtesy of Lizz Freeman, 41; © Mark Germain, 6; Courtesy of Michael Mandolfo (Forest Productions), 35; Mindy Tsonas Choi, 123; Courtesy of The Other Art Fair, Jamie Link Photography, 8, 133; Paper Jewels/Wikimedia/CC BY 4.0, 23; Courtesy of Portland Brick, 34 b.; © Raymond Boyd/Getty Images, 33; © Roger Viollet/Getty Images, 25; Salome Chasnoff, 39; © SERGEI SUPINSKY/Getty Images, 38; © Shannon Lynn Downey, 2, 108; Courtesy of Social Justice Sewing Academy, 36; © TOLGA AKMEN/Getty Images, 42; Viorella Luciana for Zeeuws Museum, courtesy of Aram Han Sifuentes, 34 t.; Courtesy of William Estrada, 30; © ZUMA Press, Inc./Alamy Stock Photo, 220
Illustrations and artwork by © Shannon Lynn Downey, unless marked otherwise in the pages

Storey books may be purchased in bulk for business, educational, or promotional use. Special editions or book excerpts can also be created to specification. For details, please contact your local bookseller or the Hachette Book Group Special Markets Department at special.markets@hbgusa.com.

Storey Publishing
210 MASS MoCA Way
North Adams, MA 01247
storey.com

Storey Publishing is an imprint of Workman Publishing, a division of Hachette Book Group, Inc., 1290 Avenue of the Americas, New York, NY 10104. The Storey Publishing name and logo are registered trademarks of Hachette Book Group, Inc.

ISBNs: 978-1-63586-890-6 (paperback); 978-1-63586-891-3 (ebook)

Printed in Canada by Transcontinental Printing on paper from responsible sources
10 9 8 7 6 5 4 3 2 1

Library of Congress Cataloging-in-Publication Data on file

the endlessly curious

THIS

the makers

BOOK

the doers

IS

the instigators

DEDICATED

the seers

TO

the lifelong learners
and all those with more questions than answers

CONT

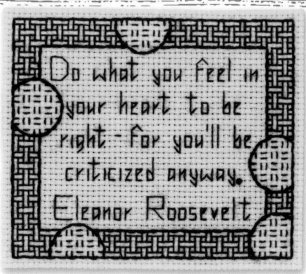

Stitched by Rosie Dickinson

MY "WHY"

Writing a book is hard. I am much more comfortable penning punchy social media posts and being able to edit and delete at any point in time. It feels like risky behavior to write a book—a work so decidedly permanent—about craftivism, which is a relatively new movement and transient by nature.

As I was writing this book, someone slid into my DMs with a thunderous attack on a thought I had about a thing, and my writing stalled. These unwelcome online interactions happen daily, and I've spent years building up calluses against them. But writing a book has made me a bit more fragile. It's impossible to think this hard, to reflect this consistently, to write down the observations and ideas that have accumulated over a decade of doing this work and not be softened and exposed. Days after my Instagram lashing, I received an unexpected piece of mail from a stitcher in the UK who is now a friend. Inside the package was a lovely note and a beautiful piece of art centering an Eleanor Roosevelt quote: "Do what you feel in your heart to be right—for you'll be criticized anyway." Bolstered by the quote and heartened by the gesture of the stitched piece (thank you, Rosie!), I returned to the computer and decided to write this preface and share my intentions for this book.

Activism is in my blood. I grew up in a proud union family that was heartily involved in the labor movement and the Democratic Party. We were on picket lines and strike lines, volunteering, and I can't even describe how exciting every voting day was. My dad has been working the polls, in his suit, for as long as I can remember. My activism took a significant feminist turn due to the Roman Catholic Church and my all-girls high school. It expanded to an intersectional awakening thanks to the glorious humans who made up the resident assistant cohort during my time at the University of Massachusetts in Amherst. It grew ever more important as I came out in college. Activism has been a metric of my growth, much like the height chart that marked my childhood bedroom door frame. I am always learning, examining, reexamining, considering, and questioning. My perspective and understanding change daily. As they should.

I came to craftivism by accident, which I'll talk about later. All good movements are dynamic, always evolving, expanding, and reshaping themselves. I believe in the power of art to create change—personal, interpersonal, institutional, and systemic—and I'm interested in the ways in which the wildly creative folks who align with craftivism as a movement can implement broader change. I cherish this community, and I'm eager to see what could happen if craftivism shifted a smidge on the spectrum, from craft-forward to activism with a side of craft. This book will explore the many ways in which the craftivism movement can grow even more prolific.

It is my hope that this book will spark ideas to feed the activism fire. It offers you strategies for ensuring maximum activist outcome while also protecting your mental health and spirit so your well doesn't run dry. You can't do everything. As with any endeavor, making a plan is key to meeting your goals. For example, if your goal is to run a marathon, you take small steps, build your strength and stamina over time, and then begin making changes to other parts of your life—what you eat, how much you sleep, how often you train—until you reach your goal. You run a 5K and then a half-marathon. Eventually, you run the marathon. But, more importantly, now you are a runner! (I have no idea why I'm using a marathon analogy. I only run when being chased, and sometimes not even then. But you get the point, and that's the point.) Even after the marathon, running remains an important part of your life.

It's the same with activism. When you commit to being a change maker, you take a step-by-step approach to the work and scale up as you learn more, find the right people to work with, and understand your own limits and boundaries. When the work is done strategically, it is generative. We don't just wake up and announce that we are going to solve the housing crisis and expect it to go well.

I don't have all the answers. No one does. I have careful observations that have come from working with tens of thousands of people in craftivism-centered spaces through my workshops and community development projects. I have training and education in formal and informal settings in the realms of activism, community organizing, marketing, and social justice mediation that all play a role in understanding how to work strategically and in collaboration. I have lived experiences that inform my place in this world and understanding of it. I bring all of it with me in creating this book.

I have many ideas to share and questions to ask. I invite you to take this journey with me.

It's party time.

i pledge allegiance

to humanity

and to the planet

we all share

one species

living under the stars

seeking love and justice

for all

LET'S GET THIS PARTY STARTED

When I was in fifth grade, my school had an art day dedicated to learning new mediums and making art. This was pretty radical for a small private Catholic school in Weymouth, Massachusetts. The majority of our extracurricular time had historically been spent attending Mass or doing service work, so an art day felt extravagant! We were able to select a few activities based on our interests, and I used a sewing machine to make a proper 1980s silk vest, which I later wore to my first concert—New Kids on the Block, of course. I also signed up to learn to cross-stitch because my favorite teacher, Mrs. Puleo, was leading that workshop. Her teaching style was very kinesthetic. It felt like nearly every lesson she taught was a craft project, and I was so totally down for it. As a student, if I was told to read something, I would read it. But if I was told to create something, I would read everything I could get my hands on about the topic so that I could create the most meaningful or clever piece of art ever made. I *loved* making things, and I was inspired to dive deeper into nearly any subject if it meant I could turn my learning into art. You should have seen my topographic map of California made with homemade playdough. Epic.

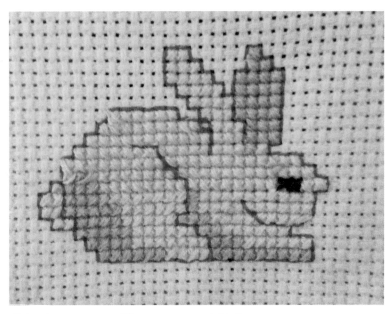

This is my very first cross-stitch.
Fifth-grade Shannon was so proud!

The cross-stitch group met in the small library on the third floor right down the hall from the teacher's lounge and the chapel. The popular screen-printing workshop was at the same time, so only four of us had signed up to cross-stitch. Mrs. Puleo had selected a pattern for us to use: a pink bunny in profile with a blue eye. I don't know about you, but I'd never seen a pink bunny with blue eyes, and I was less than excited to stitch this particular pattern. That said, I was there because I always appreciated Mrs. Puleo's classes. I was in.

To begin, Mrs. Puleo taught us how to separate our floss, thread the needle, read a pattern, and stitch. I stitched that pink bunny—half of which was stitched backward—and then glued it to a dowel, fringed the ends, and added a pink ribbon so it could hang. I gave the finished piece to my parents, and they loved it (or generously pretended to love it). It hangs in their house to this day and continues to be hideous. I did not stitch again for 20ish years.

Captain Picard saves the day (again).

In my mid-thirties, I was burned out. I had been running a digital marketing company for about eight years. I was connected to a device 24/7 because of my business, and I was desperate for a change. I happened to be scrolling through Etsy, as one does when looking to be distracted, and I stumbled upon a cross-stitch pattern of Captain Picard from *Star Trek: The Next Generation*. Have I mentioned that I am obsessed with *Star Trek TNG* and, in particular, Captain Picard? I chuckled when I saw it. I remembered the pink bunny and thought, "Well, I've done that before, and this pattern is funny, so I should buy it and make it."

That weekend, I reminded myself how to cross-stitch and stitched the most darling Captain Picard you have ever seen. The amazing part, however, was that the following day, I had my first creative idea in months. I found myself wanting to stitch something else. I was excited. I bought another Star Trek pattern and stitched again the following weekend. More good ideas came! I was onto something.

It turns out I love embroidery. The reason I didn't stitch for 20 years was not because I didn't connect with the medium but because when I learned to stitch, I didn't connect with the content. When I finally found content that spoke to me, I realized I was a stitcher at heart.

After this revelation, I quickly started to create content that naturally aligned with my work as an

Twenty years after the pink bunny, I found this pattern by Elemental Patterns and knew what needed to be done.

activist and advocate. Stitching gave me space to think substantively about the issues I was working on. At that time, my work was centered around gun violence, voter turnout, and immigration policy. I would stitch in silence and ask myself questions about the topic I was stitching on. What do I know about this? Where did that knowledge come from? Can it be trusted? What don't I know? What questions do I have? Where can I go to learn more? How do I really feel about this? Are there solutions? What do I think the root causes are? And so on.

Stitching in this way usually led to me writing about my thoughts. I began sharing my art and thoughts on Instagram to see if others wanted to engage in dialogue around these issues. Could social media be used for positive change? One particularly rough day, I stitched a handgun and talked about how utterly overwhelming it all felt. That single piece sparked my first community project to raise funds for a nonprofit in Chicago that worked with gun violence survivors. I was starting to see the potential that my art could have in galvanizing community action.

Turning Followers into Friends

My digital audience started to grow exponentially as more and more people re-grammed, retweeted, and reposted my work. But an audience of spectators was never the goal and was starting to feel uncomfortable. What I wanted were collaborators and community. So began the challenge of turning my audience into my community.

One of the fastest ways I found to expand community was to create opportunities for people to engage in projects that were joyful and easy for them—an invitation with low stakes and big outcomes. Rita's Quilt is a salient example.

The Tale of Rita's Quilt

I love a good estate sale and often find small, unfinished embroidery projects while shopping. Since I am rifling through dead people's belongings, if feels only right to buy their unfinished projects and finish them so that their souls can rest in craft peace. These are generally small projects that take under an hour to complete. I frame them and then donate them to thrift stores to finish the story of each piece.

One Sunday, I was out with my estate sale shopping crew at the last stop of the day. The minute I stepped through the door, my friend April ushered me over to the dining room to see a beautiful hand-embroidered map. It was perfectly framed and in pristine condition, and the stitching was gorgeous. The price tag said $5. I was horrified. How could something that clearly took dozens of hours to complete and had been professionally framed be disrespected like that? I bought it immediately.

I was then directed to the bedroom toward a plastic bin of what I was told were "embroidery supplies." As I started rummaging, I found a hoop, some floss, and dozens of fabric squares with patterns ironed onto them. I quickly realized I was looking at not a box of supplies but a massive embroidered quilt project. All the prep work had been done, but it lay unfinished. I exhaled a huge breath, and my friends hung their heads, knowing what was happening. I could not walk away from this.

I secretly hoped it would be too expensive to justify buying, but when I heard the price was $6, the decision was made. I took it home. As I unpacked the bin, I realized how truly massive this project was. It would take a lifetime to complete if I tried to do it alone. Also, have I mentioned that I don't quilt? I decided to call in backup and see what might happen.

I posted pictures of the quilt parts, how I had found it, and an appeal for help on Instagram. Within 24 hours, more than a thousand people had volunteered! I quickly transitioned into project manager mode, creating spreadsheets and folders and more spreadsheets. I mailed out a hundred quilt hexagons to artists across the country who each agreed to return their complete embroidered quilt pieces to me within a month.

There was an immediate groundswell of interest, enthusiasm, and support for the project and the collective journey we were embarking on. Followers wanted to know more about the person whose project we were finishing. They did some research, and we were introduced to

One hundred and thirty stitchers and sewers
came together to finish this quilt started
by Rita Smith, who had recently passed.

Rita Smith. She had passed on at the age of 99 and was an avid maker, crafter, and artist. Later, her sons would tell me she was also a feminist and would definitely have been both delighted and a bit embarrassed about all the fuss over her unfinished quilt. And so, the quilt was thereafter referred to as Rita's Quilt.

As the artists worked on their hexagons, I created a private Facebook group for them to connect with one another. They immediately began using this forum to share tips and tricks, consult on stitching styles, and get to know one another. The pieces were returned to me, and my Chicago apartment became the epicenter of all things Rita's Quilt. Approximately 30 local quilters and hand-sewers volunteered to work on the quilting portion of the project. Other volunteers came over to wash all the pieces, help me block them (a time-consuming way of stretching them while they dry to ensure they look their best), cut them to size, and prepare the entire quilt for our quilting party.

Several companies heard about the project and donated the remaining supplies we needed. A makerspace donated their shop to us for our sewing day. The quilters and sewers showed up, and in eight hours, they had hand-pieced the entire quilt top together. It was a full day of total strangers working together on a quilt meant to honor all the fiber artists throughout history whose work was never quite respected as art—to honor Rita and her incredible talent. I still get goose bumps.

At this point, in late 2016, I think I had done an interview with every press outlet on the planet about this project. A group of us took the quilt top to Los Angeles and told its story on *The Kelly Clarkson Show*. The emails, tweets, messages, and letters started pouring in. People were moved. This project was bringing back memories of their family members and ancestors. It was inspiring them to reconsider some of the handmade gifts they had been given. Beautiful stories were being shared, and strangers were connecting.

Members of the Chicago Modern Quilt Guild took over and finished the quilting and binding. The quilt debuted at a gallery in Chicago a few days before Christmas. It was displayed for only a few hours, yet hundreds showed up to see it, all of them with stories of how this project had touched them.

The quilt then traveled to Paducah, Kentucky, to the National Quilt Museum, which did a beautiful job of building out an exhibition and sharing the full story. Dozens of the artists who worked on the quilt traveled to see it with their families. We spent an entire weekend romping through Paducah and getting to know each other—and getting matching tattoos, because why not?!

Sadly, this was the weekend right before COVID-19 hit and the world shut down. The exhibition would remain dark for months. Eventually I got the quilt back, and, with permission from the other artists, I took it with me as I traveled around the country in my RV for two years. I brought the quilt to 40 states and displayed it everywhere that would have it. Many of the embroiderists who had worked on it but were unable to attend the opening in Kentucky came to see the completed quilt and share it with their communities.

This project touched millions of people. It inspired folks to think differently about fiber arts, quilting, and the artistry behind it. Rita's Quilt brought joy and hope at a very dark time. It built lifelong bonds and friendships. It demonstrated the power and potential of art in turning strangers into collaborators and friends. This is the heart of social change.

Teach me!

In the years after Rita's Quilt, I was hearing from my digital community that they wanted to try embroidering. They were curious about using a traditional handicraft with modern content. They wanted to understand how to use this medium to explore and express their opinions about issues that mattered to them, including everything from disability rights to abortion justice to mental health. This was the moment I realized that

The Other Art Fair in Chicago brought together these badass folks who arrived as strangers and left as friends.

Relationships move
at the speed of trust

Social change moves
at the speed of
relationships

Art offers us a
fast forward button

there was an incredible opportunity to help passive consumers transform into engaged makers!

Craft is the greatest tool I've ever stumbled upon for building communities and mobilizing them to take actions that will bring about actual social change. In fact, I call myself a community organizer disguised as a fiber artist. I trick people into hanging out together by promising embroidery workshops, and what we actually do is have community gatherings where we identify and find ways to work toward common goals (and also to embroider).

I started hosting little community stitch-ups in Chicago, and those workshops were nothing short of magic. Sure, many people who showed up were there to learn to embroider, but what ended up happening was that participants started connecting and having real conversations about all the things you are told never to talk about in public with strangers. Religion? Check. Politics? Definitely. Sex? You betcha! We covered it all. We were growing micro communities in the span of two hours. Reverend Jennifer Bailey said, "Relationships move at the speed of trust, but social change moves at the speed of relationships." I've never read anything that I wish I myself had thought of more than this sentence. To her statement, I would add that art offers us a fast-forward button. Strangers left these little stitch-up gatherings as community members and future friends, all because they gathered, learned something new, and built trust by being creative together. People were longing to connect, and adults especially were looking for ways to make like-minded friends. The more of these community gatherings I facilitated, the more I knew that I needed to do more.

And so I did. In the decade since that first stitch-up in Chicago, I have used every tool available to me, digital and analog, to connect people and inspire them into action. I have organized thousands of embroidery workshops, dozens of community art projects, and several global craftivism projects. I have facilitated trainings, hosted social stitching events and virtual global maker gatherings, and presented my work and philosophies to hundreds of thousands. I will dive into case studies and impact outcomes for several of these projects throughout the book to support you in your craftivism adventures. I encourage you to learn from my successes and my mistakes.

What's so special about embroidery?

The act of creating changes how people see themselves. I can't tell you how often I hear the adults in my workshops say, "But I'm not an artist" or "I can't draw" or "I am not creative." So many people have been trained to believe things about themselves that simply aren't true, and they unconsciously embrace the messages and identities they learned early in life. When folks come to a workshop, they are often profoundly anxious. They have invested their time getting educated, practicing, and challenging themselves to be excellent at a few things. They are used to being an expert and have forgotten how to be a beginner! What a gift, then, they offer simply by showing up. They are saying: Teach me something new. I'm super uncomfortable, but I'm ready to learn. It doesn't actually matter whether they fall in love with embroidery. The medium is incidental. What matters most is that they have a joyful experience being a beginner and feel encouraged and empowered to keep trying new things. Pushing through discomfort can bring about joyful transformation and remind us that change is always available to us.

To be honest, I still can't believe that embroidery has been the catalyst for so much action. But as a craftivist tool, it has all these things (and more) going for it:

1. There are virtually no barriers to entry. The materials are readily available, costs are extremely low, and you can hack materials with participants based on what they can find around their house.

2. Most anyone can learn to stitch in under an hour. They can immediately create works of art they are proud of.

3. Like most fiber art mediums, embroidery offers patterns that can be shared. New stitchers who don't identify as artists can unlearn that ingrained belief by using existing patterns to develop their artistic skills and build their creative confidence.

4. Stitching provides digital/analog balance and eases the transition for those who struggle to break free from screens. It offers the same tactile connection that we are so used to having with our digital devices.

5. Embroidery slows everything down and creates space for people to think without the pressure of immediacy. Stitching is, by nature, a slow and methodical activity and has a calming effect on both the individual and the group.

    In a group stitch-up, while everyone is working on their own pieces in parallel, conversation develops naturally and flows at a relaxed pace that mirrors the speed of stitching, which is gloriously and inherently slow. Body language that can be triggering during face-to-face conversation is removed from the equation, and because everyone is working on something, there are no expectations or awkward silences. Participants can dip in and out of a conversation, and no one thinks twice about it.

6. Embroidery lends itself nicely to online gatherings—an especially important characteristic during a pandemic, as I learned during COVID-19. I had believed stitchers need to be physically together in a room for the magic to happen. It turns out, I was absolutely wrong!

Embroidery is the bait I use to recruit people into activism. It is my siren song. The workshops and gatherings I host, in person or remotely, create a safe space where participants can get uncomfortable, reflect deeply, and connect with others. Embroidery is how I bring together strangers, turn them into communities, and encourage them to take action on the issues that matter to them.

There are, no doubt, other skills and arts with similar craftivism power. I invite you to think about what tools and expertise you have that might be used to build community and inspire people to get involved!

Inclusive Craftivism

Early in my stitching journey, I noticed that people were categorizing my work as "craftivism." It was a new word to me, and it felt like a perfect summation (craft + activism) of what I was doing: making art and art projects designed to educate, engage, and inspire the viewer around issues of social justice. However, the more I immersed myself in the craftivist community, the less I felt like I fit into it. The dominant narratives and culture of the movement chose language that offered up craftivism as a substitute to more traditional activist tactics, like protests.

In some cases, the language indicated that craftivism was an inherently more acceptable means of activism—a quiet, humble, gentle sort of activism. This framing made me physically recoil. Those very words were used by power holders in my family, community, school, and church to silence me as a girl and woman.

Activism is inherently loud, but not necessarily by volume. I can stitch something alone and in silence, as I did with my piece *Boys Will Be Boys*. It's what I call a rage stitch, one in which I just start stitching with no pattern. I sink all my rage into it. I allow the rage to be seen and felt. It is certainly not gentle, quiet, or humble. It is rarely ever pretty. But it sure can get loud.

That particular piece grew ever louder and more powerful as millions of survivors used it as the digital illustration to their #MeToo stories online. It has traveled the internet for years, going viral again and again, whenever a new high-profile perpetrator of violence and misogyny is outed. When that piece starts making the rounds on social media again, I know someone did something. Trump, Weinstein, Cosby, Kavanaugh, Lauer, Rose, Kelly, and so on. I haven't said an actual word out loud. I haven't taken to the streets with a megaphone. The piece is loud because it has impact.

When an individual shares their #MeToo story, it is anything but gentle. It's traumatic. It's brave. It's powerful. It's demonstrating how valuable and important that person's story is. It's taking up space and demanding to be seen.

The emergence and growing appeal of craftivism offers an exciting opportunity to expand how we think about activism and the many forms it can take. It is not some lesser, quieter, more thoughtful form of activism. It's a critical space within the social change ecosystem. I believe there is no voice of absolute authority in the movement, and there should be no gatekeepers. Craftivism is a powerful tool for expanding our understanding of what activism is and what it can be. It invites in new participants and offers up ways for everyone to find outlets that align with their temperament, ability, and skills both through and outside craft mediums.

Our journey begins here.

My objective in writing this book is to contribute an inclusive narrative to the ongoing cultural conversation around craftivism. I will share what I've learned while wholly dedicated to this work for 10 years (and from a lifetime as an activist), offer examples of how others are implementing their craftivism, and invite you to try things out, learn through the process, and expand and grow the movement. I hope you find it a helpful tool in your activism journey! The first part of the book will introduce you to craftivism and provide some historical context. We then explore the hard work of self-reflection that is a critical part of an activist's journey. From there, we will dive into a strategic path for centering activism in your craftivism practice, from identifying symptoms and root causes to recruiting collaborators. Throughout, we will examine case studies to put a face to the work. We will also reframe our understanding of activism in service to protecting your health and sanity while engaged in this challenging but vital work. The final chapter is a robust planning template for use in building out your future craftivism projects, actions, or responses. The document will guide you in applying everything you have learned throughout the book to the issues you care most about.

A willingness to try new things is the seed that can sprout new ideas, creativity, and, most importantly, curiosity. Together we have the capacity to fundamentally reimagine everything. And that is exactly what we need right now. What better way to expand thinking than by developing a creative practice? Creativity breeds hope.

I am thrilled that you are here and reading this book. It is my sincerest hope that you will find value, inspiration, helpful tools, and encouragement. Mostly, I hope these thoughts and examples expand the conversation around what it means to be an activist, an art activist, and a craftivist.

I believe in the power of the individual and the exponential power of community as agents of change. From a single action to a lifetime of actions, it all counts and it all matters. I believe in you, and I don't say that lightly. You are here and open to new ideas. That is one of the most important attributes of an activist.

The social change ecosystem is vast and wide, and when contributions and efforts align, change happens at a much faster pace. Art can be an astoundingly powerful complement to social change movements, particularly when it's in collaboration with other activism tactics and built around strategy and vision. It's all important. We can all be valuable contributors.

"DON'T MAKE ME REPEAT MYSELF."

-HISTORY

CHAPTER 1

WHAT'S OLD IS NEW AGAIN

A DIVE INTO THE HISTORY OF CRAFTIVISM

While the term *craftivism* (*craft* + *activism*) is relatively new, introduced by Betsy Greer in 2003, the use of art and craft as tools for activism has been in play for a very long time. You've likely heard of the pink pussyhat, which served as a symbol of resistance during the Women's March of 2017. But are you familiar with the ancient Roman pileus cap? Given to formerly enslaved people, it was a hand-felted hat that became a symbol of liberty and was later adopted by French and American revolutionaries during their respective wars for liberation. And that is just the start! We will explore the deep historical roots of creative mediums used as activist tools alongside contemporary initiatives throughout this chapter.

In terms of the current movement, Greer provided a word and framing that modern makers could unite around and identify with, and since then the definition of craftivism has continued to evolve. It has been expanded, shaped, and reshaped based on the growth of the community, the ongoing examination of the history of art activism, the evolution of the uses of craft in activism, and the growing diversity of voices and mediums taking part in the movement. I currently define craftivism as an independent or collective art practice meant to build power and agency in direct support of actions aimed at creating social or political change. As a fiber artist, I lean on textiles and fiber as the creative tools of my craftivism work. But one of the wonderfully inclusive qualities of craftivism is that it is in no way limited to any particular medium. All art is welcome and needed. Craftivism is an open invitation to anyone who wants to participate, whatever their temperament, ability, and skill in their medium of choice.

A perfect example is Girls Garage, a California-based nonprofit founded by Emily Pilloton-Lam that is changing the landscape of who designs our material world. Girls Garage provides girls and gender-expansive youth ages 9 to 18 with free and low-cost programs in carpentry, architecture, engineering, welding, and art activism. The 300 students enrolled in the program each year craft everything from feminist safety signs to epic pride parade floats and garden boxes to support Feed Black Futures. To help fire you up and get you thinking about ways you can use your craft to take action in support of issues that matter most to you, we will explore the work of other boundary-pushing initiatives like Girls Garage that challenge folks to engage in activism in a hands-on way.

Let's get organized.

The key to successful craftivism is ensuring that the activism within the practice is present, clear, and articulated. The foundation of that activism is built on power building, action, and outcomes.

Humans love to put things into categories in an effort to make order out of chaos. We can't help ourselves, and I am not immune. Following are some categories and loose definitions for various approaches to art and craft activism and initiatives that I find interesting or particularly effective. Many projects fall into several categories, and the list is in no way finite or rigid, but it helps give a sense of the general landscape of the evolving craftivism movement.

AWARENESS. A piece, collection of pieces, or project designed to bring attention to an issue or topic that is not widely known or understood.

BOYCOTT. A project whose objective is to encourage the intentional and voluntary refusal to buy or use a product or have dealings with a person, organization, or location as an expression of protest. In the realm of craftivism, a boycott can often involve the substitution of a commercial/industrial product with a handmade item.

CHALLENGING NARRATIVES. A piece, collection of pieces, or project designed to produce and spread counternarratives to problematic dominant narratives.

CIVIC ENGAGEMENT. A piece, collection of pieces, or project designed to inspire, equip, and encourage individuals to take action on an issue of public concern.

CODED MESSAGE SHARING. A piece or collection of pieces created to secretly share information with a specific community or audience.

COMMUNITY BUILDING. A project whose objective is to bring people together, either digitally or in person, around a shared need or interest.

EDUCATION. A piece, collection of pieces, or project created for the purpose of sharing knowledge with the viewer or community.

HEALING. A piece, collection of pieces, or project meant to aid in a physical, mental, or spiritual healing journey.

IDENTITY/ALLEGIANCE SIGNALING. The creation of a handmade item with a significant meaning that becomes a symbol for a movement, identity, action, or cause by demonstrating alignment and allegiance.

A WORD ABOUT AWARENESS . . .

Australian comedian Hannah Gadsby talks about "pufferfish moments"—those little triggering moments in life that cause you to puff up because you have big feelings about something. (If you haven't seen their show *Douglas*, please do. Gadsby is brilliant beyond words.) I've learned that my own pufferfish moments mostly occur around awareness campaigns.

Many craftivism projects are centered on spreading awareness about a particular issue. That is awesome when most people are not aware of the issue and you want to bring it into their consciousness. The first step toward changing things is to make as many people as possible aware of the issue. It is extra awesome when you can both bring the issue into their awareness and ask them to do something about it—learn more, sign a petition, vote a certain way, show up for an event, et cetera.

However, when an awareness campaign is centered on an issue that most people are already aware of, it feels at best wildly ineffective and at worst performative. For example, in the United States, we are all painfully aware of gun violence. We breathe that air every single day. We do not need awareness campaigns about gun violence. Instead, we need action-oriented projects to inspire folks who feel totally powerless to do anything about it to contribute to the change.

PHILANTHROPY. A piece, collection of pieces, or project created with the intention of raising money to resource a specific need, cause, individual, or organization.

PROTEST. A piece, collection of pieces, or project where the outcome centers a statement or action that offers up critique, objection, disapproval, or a counternarrative to an issue or topic.

RECORD KEEPING. A piece, collection of pieces, or project meant to create a material record of something deemed important by the instigator, its physical form giving it permanence.

REFLECTION AND UNDERSTANDING. A piece, collection of pieces, or project whose intention is to create space for self-reflection, growth, personal understanding, healing, and agency.

RESISTANCE. A piece, collection of pieces, or project that serves to undermine, sabotage, refuse compliance, or prevent something from happening.

RESOURCE BUILDING. A project that invites makers to contribute goods and items to build resources around a specific community need.

SKILL SHARING. A community gathering, in person or digital, in which folks willingly trade their knowledge and skills without expectation of reimbursement.

SOCIAL AND POLITICAL COMMENTARY. A piece, collection of pieces, or project designed to offer rhetorical analysis and commentary on an issue of social or political importance.

STORYTELLING. A piece, collection of pieces, or project that exists to share lived experiences and cultural truths.

STREET CRAFTIVISM. A piece, collection of pieces, or project that exists in public space, is meant to draw attention to a cause or issue, and may or may not be sanctioned for display.

Take a look.
It's in a book.

Art and artists have always been at the forefront of politics, religion, activism, and resistance, from the Roman pileus cap to Ai Weiwei's *Study of Perspective—Tiananmen Square* to the Guerrilla Girls. Here are some examples of craftivism from throughout history. These should provide some context as we start to think about the ways we use art as an activism tool. If these snippets inspire or resonate with you, go explore them—go deep into the magic rabbit hole of the internet to see what other treasures you uncover.

Pileus/Liberty Caps

In the later years of the Roman Empire, the pileus cap was gifted to and worn by formerly enslaved people when they were liberated. It symbolized their freedom and their right to vote (provided they were male). Later, the hat became a symbol of the end of the dictatorship of Caesar. The idea of this handmade cap as a symbol of freedom evolved and morphed into the liberty caps worn as symbols of allegiance during the American Revolutionary War and later the French Revolution. In fact, hats and other garments have been symbols of resistance, allegiance, and identity throughout history.

CRAFTIVISM CATEGORIES: identity/allegiance, civic engagement, awareness

Anna Maria Radclyffe

Imagine it's 1716, and your 26-year-old husband has just been beheaded for his role in the Scottish Jacobite rebellion. How do you begin to process such a thing? Anna Maria Radclyffe picked up a needle and copious amounts of hair and stitched a memorial into her husband's prison bedsheets. It reads, "The sheet off my dear, dear Lord's Bed in the wretched Tower of London February 1716 x Ann C of Darwent = Waters †." Experts suggest that the hair was likely hers, her husband's, or a combination of the two. In 2022, the art was displayed in the Museum of London. Anna made sure her and her husband's love and legacy of resistance lived on.

CRAFTIVISM CATEGORIES: record keeping, protest, storytelling, healing

Swadeshi Movement

A key component of the Indian independence movement was the Swadeshi movement. This "Make in India" campaign, initiated in 1905, was an economic boycott of goods manufactured or imported by the British, with the ultimate goal of national self-sufficiency and self-governance. It was especially focused on textiles and included a push to return to precolonial traditional Indian dress. Led by Mahatma Gandhi,

spinning centers across the country coordinated in producing textiles for clothing, and spinners were largely considered freedom fighters. The spinning wheel became the symbol of the movement and can be found as the central image on the Indian flag today.

CRAFTIVISM CATEGORIES: boycott, protest, resource building, community building, skill sharing, resistance, healing

The Red Cross
During World Wars I and II, the American Red Cross facilitated massive campaigns to engage those at home in the creation of resources for the armed forces. Thousands of Americans of all ages knit millions of socks, sweaters, mufflers, blankets, helmet liners, and wristlets, in accordance with the stringent guidelines established by the Red Cross in collaboration with the US military.

CRAFTIVISM CATEGORIES: resource building, skill sharing, community building, civic engagement

Phyllis Latour Doyle

Phyllis Latour Doyle was a British secret agent working in France against the Nazis during World War II, and her story is the stuff of movies and legends. As a spy, she was able to transmit 135 secret messages to London from behind enemy lines to guide bombing missions. She explained how she concealed her codes: "I always carried knitting because my codes were on a piece of silk—I had about 2,000 I could use. When I used a code, I would just pinprick it to indicate it had gone. I wrapped the piece of silk around a knitting needle and put it in a flat shoelace which I used to tie my hair up." In 2014, Phyllis was awarded France's highest military honor, the Legion of Honor, for her spycraft.

CRAFTIVISM CATEGORIES: coded message sharing, resistance

The Ghost Army

During World War II, a top-secret unit of approximately 1,100 officers and men were tasked with outsmarting the Nazis. This group of artists, engineers, and soldiers made up the first tactical deception unit. (How cool is that name?) They created a robust multimedia mobile installation that included inflatable tanks and vehicles, fake radio traffic, sound

effects, and phony generals. They duped German forces into believing the Allied forces had placed troops in places where they hadn't. They had the capacity to simulate two full units—approximately 30,000 men—with their artistry and craft. They were credited with saving thousands of lives and playing an important role in the Allied victory. Their creative trickery stayed classified until the mid-1990s.

CRAFTIVISM CATEGORY: resistance

NAMES Project AIDS Memorial Quilt

In the early years of the AIDS epidemic, power holders in the United States harbored a great deal of antipathy toward the disease because it was seen as a "gay plague." In fact, though the epidemic began in 1981, President Ronald Reagan didn't even speak publicly about it until 1985. At that point it had already killed 3,500 people. By 1987, the year the memorial quilt was first displayed, 47,000 people had died of AIDS.

The AIDS quilt brought global attention and awareness to the issue and was a key contribution to the activism that forced the US government to finally take action. The quilt was the brainchild of activist Cleve Jones. At an annual candlelight march honoring Harvey Milk and

George Moscone, Jones asked participants to write the names of people they had lost to AIDS on placards. These were then taped to the San Francisco Federal Building. This visual inspired him. A small group got together to plan a more significant and permanent memorial to the lives lost. Each quilt panel honors the life of one person lost to AIDS.

The quilt was first displayed in October 1987 on the National Mall during the National March on Washington for Lesbian and Gay Rights. There were 1,920 panels. The quilt then went on a 20-city national tour and raised nearly half a million dollars for AIDS organizations. The quilt is now made up of more than 50,000 panels, weighs 54 tons, and is housed in San Francisco. It still tours as a teaching tool and exhibition.

CRAFTIVISM CATEGORIES: awareness, protest, resistance, record keeping, community building, education, civic engagement, storytelling, social and political commentary, reflection and understanding, healing, street craftivism, philanthropy

The Guerrilla Girls

The Guerrilla Girls are a group of art activists who have by and large remained anonymous since the mid-1980s, seen only while wearing

gorilla masks. This crew has been throwing down against "gender and ethnic bias and corruption in art, film, politics, and pop culture," according to their website, using any artistic means necessary, from posters to projections. Their guerrilla work has been so effective and powerful that many of the art institutions they challenge have invited them in. Their art activism has quite literally forced the entire fine art community to take a long hard look at how and why they make the choices they do. (It's hard for me to quantify just how much I love and admire their work.)

CRAFTIVISM CATEGORIES: protest, education, civic engagement, resistance, challenging narratives, storytelling, social and political commentary, street craftivism, awareness

Angel Action

In 1998, college student Matthew Shepard was tortured and brutally murdered in a hate crime in Laramie, Wyoming, for being gay. The impact and media coverage of his murder was profound and generated a great deal of public sentiment. In response, Fred Phelps and the Westboro Baptist Church protested Matthew's funeral en masse. They carried signs with messages of hate, including "God hates fags."

Matthew's friend Romaine Patterson (now an LGBTQ activist) was at the funeral and wanted to do something as a counterprotest to the anti-gay protest. She organized Angel Action, a group of activists who built and wore massive white angel wings and used them to block protestors from sight at the trial of Matthew's killers. Since then, the angels have donned their wings to protect queer community gatherings across the country, such as mourners of the Pulse nightclub mass shooting in Orlando, Florida, in 2016. They share the instructions for making the angel wings freely online.

CRAFTIVISM CATEGORIES: street craftivism, protest, community building, resistance, healing

The Red Thread Project

Conceived and led by artist (and my friend) Lindsay Obermeyer, the Red Thread Project ran from 2004 to 2020, when Lindsay passed. On her website, Lindsay described her vision for the Red Thread Project: "This beautiful project celebrated the visible (and invisible) connections within community while simultaneously creating resources for the unhoused, elderly, children in the foster care system, and those fighting cancer." The project involved the creation of thousands of knit and crochet hats by community members. The hats were then attached to a half-mile-long red thread. Community members gathered, wore the connected hats, and exhibited them through a performance. The hats were then donated to local charities.

CRAFTIVISM CATEGORIES: resource building, community building, skill sharing, street craftivism

Operations Christmas and Rivers of Light

There are many examples of wartime craftivism, but Operation Christmas and Operation Rivers of Light are two examples of activism aimed at ending war. From 2010 to 2012, the Colombian military partnered with an advertising agency in an attempt to end their civil war. Their goal was to bring guerrilla fighters out of the jungles and reintegrate them into their families and communities through the support of job training and psychological support. During Operation Christmas, the military chose a path widely used by guerrilla fighters and brought Christmas to the jungle by decorating the trees with lights and messages that invited and encouraged them to come home. The result was 331 people demobilizing. This inspired the next action, Operation Rivers of Light, which invited family and friends who lived near conflict areas to write Christmas letters to their loved ones asking them to come home. The letters were placed in illuminated floating balls and sent down the river. The result: 180 additional guerrilla fighters demobilized.

CRAFTIVISM CATEGORIES: healing, community building, challenging narratives, social and political commentary, street craftivism, awareness

The Mobile Street Art Cart

One of the brilliant initiatives of Chicago artist and educator William Estrada is the mobile street art cart. The cart, which mirrors a food vendor cart and can be pushed by hand or pulled by a bike, brings free art projects to the communities of Chicago. William's cart can handle myriad mediums, from screen printing to button making. On his website, William describes the mission of the project: "The Mobile Street Art Cart amplifies the creativity that already exists in our communities by addressing relevant social issues through art making in the streets." Personally, I want to see art carts in every community around the world.

CRAFTIVISM CATEGORIES: community building, civic engagement, education, skill sharing, challenging narratives, storytelling, social and political commentary, street craftivism

Project FIRE

Project FIRE (Fearless, Initiative, Recovery, Empowerment) is a trauma recovery program built around craftivism for youth injured by gun violence in Chicago. Each day in the program begins with three hours of glassblowing, followed by an hour of youth-cofacilitated trauma-informed support groups. The young artists are able to sell their work and participate in wholesale product fulfillment to develop their economic independence and entrepreneurial skills. The initiative includes an employment and mentorship program.

CRAFTIVISM CATEGORIES: community building, healing, education, civic engagement, skill sharing, challenging narratives, reflection and understanding

Mimes against White Supremacy

You heard me. I said mimes against white supremacy. In 2010, staff at the Center for New Community (CNC) learned of a plan by the anti-immigrant group NumbersUSA to attend an immigrant rights march in Washington, DC. NumbersUSA staff were planning to attend the march with cameras in the hope of livestreaming while they engaged unsuspecting marchers in debates that would portray immigration rights advocates in a negative light. The CNC team met the group at the march dressed as mimes, blowing whistles and carrying balloons, to interrupt their plans and encourage marchers not to engage with them. They were successful in preventing the NumbersUSA team from being able to carry out their plans, and their artistic antics earned them national press, bringing further attention to the underhanded plans of the xenophobic white supremacist organization.

CRAFTIVISM CATEGORIES: protest, civic engagement, challenging narratives, resistance, street craftivism

Tattoos for Change

Quite a few tattoo artists provide free services to those in need. They include Gloria Juarez, a Houston-based artist and entrepreneur who provides free areola tattoos to breast cancer survivors. Maryland-based artist Dave Cutlip provides free cover-up tattoos for folks with racist, bigoted, or gang-related tattoos. Other examples abound.

CRAFTIVISM CATEGORY: healing

Blue Tin Production

Founded by Hoda Katebi, Blue Tin Production is working to revolutionize the fashion industry at the manufacturing level. This Chicago-based worker-owned, worker-run cooperative does all cutting and sewing in-house and with no minimum order requirements, and it focuses on sustainability and centering the circular economy. The co-op team members are all people who are women of color, trans, gender nonconforming, intergenerational, queer, working class, immigrants, and/or refugees. According to the co-op's website, all workers receive health care, mental health support, access to social services, paid professional development, on-site interpreters, childcare, educational and wellness training, and a community devoted to supporting one another.

CRAFTIVISM CATEGORIES: community building, education, skill sharing, challenging narratives, resource building, social and political commentary

Stop Telling Women to Smile

Brooklyn-based artist Tatyana Fazlalizadeh offers a dynamic street craftivism campaign titled Stop Telling Women to Smile, which boldly tackles gender-based street harassment in public spaces. The campaign uses posters showing drawn portraits of women in combination with captions that speak directly to the verbal harassment women experience in public, directly challenging offenders in the very same spaces where they typically offend. The project is now documented and contextualized in a book of the same title.

CRAFTIVISM CATEGORIES: street craftivism, protest, resistance, challenging narratives, social and political commentary

Protest Banner Lending Library

Started by artist Aram Han Sifuentes, the Protest Banner Lending Library is just that: a collection of more than 600 banners that can be borrowed, used, and returned. The banners are created through community workshops where participants learn the ins and outs of banner making, protesting, and community mobilizing. More than 3,000 banners have been created through the project. The lending library has created a way for those who cannot participate in street protest to come together, connect, and contribute.

CRAFTIVISM CATEGORIES: protest, community building, record keeping, civic engagement, resistance, skill sharing, resource building, social and political commentary, healing, street craftivism

Portland Brick Project

Community members in Portland, Maine, were provided an opportunity to claim and redefine their city history through this literal street art craftivism project. Folks were invited to submit historical and personal facts that occurred within the city's India Street neighborhood. These moments were then marked by the creation of stamped bricks, handmade using local clay, that were inserted into the city's brick sidewalks to commemorate what happened "on this spot." Each location connects to an online map and audio tour available through the project's website.

CRAFTIVISM CATEGORIES: community building, record keeping, story-telling, social and political commentary, street craftivism, awareness

Stitch Buffalo

Stitch Buffalo is a nonprofit in Buffalo, New York, that has created a textile art center showcasing the incredible skill and artistry of the community's refugee and immigrant women. Here more than 55 women artists from Bhutan, Burma, Nepal, Thailand, Egypt, Afghanistan, and beyond sew handcrafted goods for sale in the community through the Refugee Women's Workshop. The center also offers community educa-tion, inviting folks into their space to learn from their members through workshops covering everything from embroidery to weaving. I highly recommend doing some online shopping with them! The artistry is mind-blowing.

CRAFTIVISM CATEGORIES: community building, edu-cation, skill sharing, story-telling, resource building, reflection and understand-ing, healing

Social Justice Sewing Academy

The Social Justice Sewing Academy (SJSA) works to support young people in matters of self-expression and social change through quilting and textile arts. In classrooms and community spaces, this program offers young people the opportunity to explore and express themselves as thinkers and advocates. They translate their ideas into quilt squares, and those squares are then compiled into stunning community quilts, often with the support of skilled embroidery artists from across the country. The academy has grown and expanded to include memorial and remembrance quilts that honor the victims of violence. They have created an antiracist guidebook and a business incubator for young social justice entrepreneurs. Their work continues to disrupt the quilting world in all the best ways.

CRAFTIVISM CATEGORIES: education, community building, protest, record keeping, civic engagement, resistance, skill sharing, challenging narratives, storytelling, resource building, social and political commentary, reflection and understanding, healing, awareness

Welcome Blanket Project

The Welcome Blanket Project invites makers to create a blanket that is gifted to new immigrants as a way of welcoming them to the United States and their new communities here. The blankets are presented to recipients through refugee resettlement groups and include letters of welcome. Before being gifted to their recipients, the blankets are exhibited at art institutions throughout the country, amplifying the message of support and welcome for immigrants and refugees as well as recruiting new makers as contributors.

CRAFTIVISM CATEGORIES: community building, education, storytelling, resource building, social and political commentary, awareness

Knit for Food

Instigated by fiber artist Laura Nelkin, Knit for Food was a 12-hour knit-a-thon to raise money for and awareness of food insecurity. (Yes, it was inspired by an episode of *Gilmore Girls* . . . there's inspiration everywhere!) Participants invited their communities to sponsor them for every hour they knit to raise money. There were 12 hours of online programming scheduled for participants as well. This ranged from presentations to dance parties to guided yoga and stretching and even stitch lounges, where people from around the world could get to know each other while they stitched. The 2022 event raised $271,671, which was divided evenly across four nonprofits working to end hunger.

CRAFTIVISM CATEGORIES: philanthropy, awareness, community building, education

War in Ukraine

In 2022, the first few months of the war in Ukraine gave us examples of craftivism both in-country and around the world. Hundreds of Ukrainian civilians came together to weave camouflage tents and walls to hide tanks, supplies, and soldiers from Russian military forces. Metal artists, welders, and construction crews created massive antitank obstacles called hedgehogs to protect the city of Kyiv. Around the world, artists and activists took action to raise money through craft-based projects. My favorite act of international artistic resistance was in Lisbon, Portugal, where activists used projectors to light up the Russian embassy with the colors of the Ukrainian flag.

CRAFTIVISM CATEGORIES: protest, resistance, resource building, social and political commentary, street craftivism, awareness

Gone But Not Forgotten

A collaboration between artist Rachel Wallis and the Chicago grassroots collective We Charge Genocide, Gone But Not Forgotten is a community quilting project that documents the individuals killed by the Chicago Police Department or while in police custody from 2006 to 2016. The group facilitated 15 peace/quilting circles where participants read the names and stories of victims aloud while hand-stitching a quilt square in their memory. These visual stories were then quilted into panels, stretching nearly 40 feet in length and honoring 144 victims. These events provided a safe space for people from all over Chicago to gather and talk about police accountability, transformative justice, and community safety. Having been fortunate enough to participate in one, I can testify to the impact and importance of these gatherings. On her website, Rachel shares, "Gone But Not Forgotten appears to be the most comprehensive public collection of information about who has been killed by the police in Chicago. The names, ages, and dates of death featured on the quilt panels, as well as the victim information sheets collected in the binders on display, were gathered through a combination of official police records, newspaper articles, and information from victims' families. Many of the victims' names and stories remain unknown."

CRAFTIVISM CATEGORIES: community building, record keeping, education, civic engagement, skill sharing, challenging narratives, awareness, healing

Breonna Taylor Postcard Campaign

In March 2020, Breonna Taylor, a young Black woman, was shot and killed in her own home, unarmed, by police in Louisville, Kentucky. In September of that year, activist-artist Melissa Blount engaged community to raise awareness around this horrific murder, highlighting the lack of integrity and inaction of former Kentucky Attorney General Daniel Cameron to file charges against the Louisville police officers. Led by Melissa (with support from other craftivists, including me), contributors held online postcard-making sewing circles, while dozens of people gathered at Colvin House in Chicago to sew in person. The community created more than a hundred handmade postcards, which they mailed to Cameron's home.

CRAFTIVISM CATEGORIES: protest, community building, record keeping, civic engagement, resistance, skill sharing, challenging narratives, social and political commentary, awareness

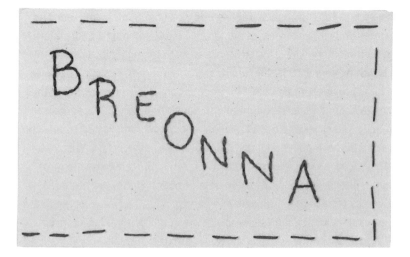

Tehachapi

A project led by artist JR, Tehachapi brought a massive installation inside the walls of the California prison of the same name. JR and his team spent time with current and former inmates and staff to learn about their lives and experiences. The participants were photographed, and a collage was then printed and installed in the prison yard. The exhibit is 183,000 square feet in size, and the entire process took only a few hours. As JR explains, "The form gave voice to those locked in a system that does not otherwise offer them one." A drone was used to photograph the installed piece, and, importantly, an app was created to share the installation and the personal stories of each of the 48 inmates who make up the exhibit.

CRAFTIVISM CATEGORIES: community building, record keeping, resistance, challenging narratives, storytelling, social and political commentary, street craftivism, awareness

RicRACK

RicRACK is a creative reuse shop and community sewing studio based in New Orleans, Louisiana. Its supplies and product inventory are donated by film and television productions as well as the local community. RicRACK offers community textile recycling in addition to a vast array of workshops aimed at fostering waste reduction, sustainability, creative expression, and entrepreneurship. It also does its part to make Mardi Gras more sustainable by offering handmade throws and upcycled costuming and decorations.

CRAFTIVISM CATEGORIES: community building, education, skill sharing, resource building, street craftivism

Little Amal

Little Amal is a 12-foot puppet created by the Handspring Puppet Company of South Africa for the performance art project The Walk. The puppet plays the part of a 10-year-old Syrian refugee and represents the vast number of children fleeing war and violence today. Little Amal has traveled the world over, including a massive trek across the United

States in 2023. The puppeteers hand out donation postcards to the crowds that come to see her. Beyond bringing attention to the plight of young refugees and displaced youth, her "walks" have raised hundreds of thousands of dollars for education, food, shelter, emergency medical care, and legal assistance for refugees around the world.

CRAFTIVISM CATEGORIES: community building, education, civic engagement, challenging narratives, storytelling, social and political commentary, street craftivism, philanthropy, awareness

A Movement with Momentum: Everyone Is Invited

Art and craft are older than the written word. It is no wonder diverse mediums have served as tools for change makers throughout history. As you've seen from the brief survey in this chapter, craft-supported activism has been in play far longer than the term *craftivism*. With this new term and the birth of the modern craftivism movement, a powerful legion of crafters and makers has been ushered into the world of activism. Craftivism has unlocked a pathway for artists and creators working in various mediums to explore their activist identities and how they can channel their work toward actions that support their values and beliefs. The activist journey is lifelong and rooted in self-reflection, curiosity, and strategy. I invite you to jump into the deep end with me, get comfortable being uncomfortable, and do some hard work that will literally change your life. Sound a bit scary? I promise there is fun to be had.

mind the gap
between your
values and actions

CHAPTER 2

I PUT THE FUN IN UNCOMFORTABLE

WANT TO CHANGE THE WORLD? DEAL WITH YOUR SHIT.

How we self-identify, what we believe about ourselves, and what values we hold form the foundation of everything we do in this world—how we interact with others and how we respond to their actions, beliefs, and words. Effective and powerful activists are confident in the identities they hold. The bedrock of their strength is comfort and confidence in their beliefs, which fuels their drive to close the gap between their values and their actions. For example, many animal rights activists choose to adhere to a plant-based diet and buy vegan-friendly clothing that is either plant-based or synthetic. These actions align with their core values and support businesses whose ethics are, in turn, aligned with those of the animal rights movement.

Activists who hold this understanding stand firm in their values and make decisions that reinforce those values—even when it is difficult or inconvenient or it proves costly. We do this by asking ourselves the hard questions, examining our identities and privileges, and critically exploring our own beliefs. We do this over and over again, daily. It is a lifelong journey, and it is not restricted to activists. Think back through your own life and the moments that challenged the strength of your convictions: When you witnessed one of your classmates being bullied and had to decide whether to saddle up with the popular kids or defend the person being bullied. The pressure to have sex when you weren't sure you were ready. Advocating for yourself with a health care provider who wasn't hearing you. Addressing or ignoring the racist comment in the lunchroom at your workplace. We encounter these pivot points every day, and they all matter because they construct the scaffolding of our identities. The more confident we can become about who we are, the easier it is to move through these moments with grace and tenacity.

Years ago there was a moment when, despite desperately needing money, I turned down an offer of work because it was not in alignment with my values. My ex had left me in an impossible financial situation. The project I was offered was a short-term and well-paying one-off that no one would have known I was involved in. But the gig was for a pharmaceutical company that was causing harm to people through its pricing, patent control, and business practices. Despite that, I met with the company rep, considered the offer, and wrestled with my soul and my needs for days before ultimately turning down the job. I cried a lot, out of both despair and relief. I would not have been able to live with myself if I had taken it.

A few days later, I got an unexpected call from a social enterprise doing magnificent work in service to a more equitable society. My soul yelled *Yes!* Had I accepted the pharmaceutical job, I would not have had the bandwidth to say yes to this opportunity that fully aligned with my values. It was a turning point. Once I decided to no longer consider job offers that were at odds with my values, more prospects that aligned with my beliefs presented themselves, and I eventually found myself in a community and network of like-minded individuals.

Opportunities continued to materialize, and soon enough, I was in a position where I could pay it forward and create opportunities for others. Don't get me wrong—I am still learning, growing, and always striving to close the gap between my values and actions. It's an active, lifelong process, and it isn't easy. It's uncomfortable to check in with yourself often, ask the hard questions, and hold yourself accountable to what you value and believe in. I exist in a calmer, happier, and more aligned way than ever before because of my commitment to doing the work of dealing with my own shit so I can more effectively work in service of others and the issues that matter to me.

Let's talk about triggers.

Money used to be one of my biggest triggers. I grew up on the poor side of working class, which eventually transitioned to run-of-the-mill working class. I was conditioned to believe that we never had enough (and we never would) and that people with money were always exploitative and untrustworthy. Of course, none of this was or is true, but classist thinking was strong during my formative years.

Money became a terrible tension point in my relationships. I always wanted to carry half of the financial burden (half of the rent, half of the monthly grocery bills, and so on) because that is how I perceived equity, despite being with partners who took in way more money than I did. I found talking about money with a partner to be a debilitating experience, and I refused to acknowledge this until the tension grew too strong to ignore. I started seeing a wonderful therapist whom I felt seen and supported by. We spent months unpacking how society, the church, my family, ex partners, and my ego played powerful roles in my understanding of and relationship to money. I also worked with a financial adviser to help me set up systems, and his morally neutral approach to finances as a tool that could be used in positive ways had a huge impact on how I perceived money. It sounds like such a simple paradigm shift, and yet it took time and a lot of deeply uncomfortable work for me to get there.

These experiences fundamentally changed how I think about money, how I acquire money, and the value of money in my life. Now most of my work is done on a pay-what-you-can basis. In this way, money is not a barrier to people engaging with my work, and at the same time, those who can pay more do. It is quite beautiful, and while my income is never predictable, that doesn't carry the same stress it might have in the past. I know my personal value, and the value of my work isn't directly correlated to how much money I make. It's another step toward freedom for me.

Why do I tell you all this? So that you can see that personal development is a journey. That it's hard. You will face setbacks. Mostly, I hope you see how very worthwhile it is. Don't let fear hold you back. Question everything you think you know, and see what comes of it. I'm here to support you.

Game on!

The following series of activities will lay the groundwork for your exploration and self-strengthening practice. I do many of them regularly and find that I learn something new about myself each time.

These activities are meant to help you find some starting points—places from where you can move forward in the work of unlearning and growth. The best part is that when you revisit them, months or years later, they will provide you with new starting points. It's the uncomfortable gift that keeps on giving.

YES, NO, MAYBE SO

Make three columns on a piece of blank paper. At the top of each column, write . . .

WHo I DEFiNiTELY AM	WHo I DEFiNiTELY AM NOT	WHo I MiGHT BE
Write at least 10 words that absolutely, without a doubt, describe you. These can be identities, descriptors, personality traits, or anything you feel supremely confident about.	Write 10 words you feel strongly do not describe you.	This column will likely be the most challenging. Write 10 words that might describe you, even if you don't feel 100 percent confident owning them just yet. These could also be words you would like to describe you as well as those that you don't want to own but might describe you anyway.

READY? GO! Spend some time with your lists. Put a star next to things that feel good to know about yourself. Add a question mark to things that cause you to pause and think. Hang up your list in a spot where you can see it often.

SHARE WITH OTHERS. Talk about the list with friends, family, teachers, clergy, your therapist—anyone whose opinion you value. Ask for feedback. What do the people in your life see in your list? What do they see in you that you didn't write down? Use this exercise to open a dialogue with yourself and others about your identities and how they make you feel. Importantly, don't judge yourself. Explore and stay curious, but try not to be critical of yourself. If you wrote down something that doesn't feel good, get in there and poke it. Why does it feel bad or uncomfortable to you? What can you do to change it?

DO IT AGAIN LATER. Try this activity again in a few months. Don't refer to your previous lists; start fresh. How does it feel this time? Compare your new list to your previous results. What has changed? What trends can you spot?

PAIR UP. Sometimes we need another perspective to do this self-reflective work. For example, you might try doing this exercise with a partner. Invite a person who knows you well and whom you trust to fill out the lists on your behalf. Compare your list with theirs. I guarantee they will see things in you that you didn't see in yourself. What can these new insights teach you? How might they impact your sense of self, the identities you currently hold, or even the identities you aspire to hold?

HOW UNCOMFORTABLE ARE YOU WILLING TO GET IN SERVICE TO A JUST WORLD?

IDEAL SELF

Don't you love when you bring your best self to the table? Building off your Yes, No, Maybe So lists, take a stab at articulating what your best-self vibe is.

PROMPT: When I show up as my best self,
- I feel like . . .
- I act like . . .
- I interact with others like . . .
- I sound like . . .
- I look like . . .

This can be challenging. Here's what mine looked like.

When I show up as my best self, on the other side of money fear:
- I feel free of the constant fear of not having enough money.
- I act with a calm confidence, knowing that my self-worth is not defined by my financial success.
- I interact with others like I am not constrained by my fears about not contributing enough or not being compensated enough.
- I sound like someone who knows their value and asks for it with confidence; will say no to accepting less; is clear about what they need and is satisfied with having enough; and will talk about money with transparency and without unnecessary emotion.
- I look like someone who has always found a way and therefore does not need to carry fear around with me.

Guess what? I am all those things now. I just gave myself a high-five like Liz Lemon.

TELL ME ABOUT ME

You will interview your loved ones about you in this activity. When I say loved ones, I mean just that: people who love you and will be generous and real with you in service to your journey. Trust your gut. Invite them to sit down for a quick interview about how they see you. You are the interviewer and the topic!

QUESTIONS TO GET YOU STARTED

- What do you think I'm good at?
- What do you love about me?
- What makes me laugh?
- What is one of your favorite memories of me/us?
- Tell me my story in one minute or less.
- What songs remind you of me?

Now come up with your own questions!

Get curious about identity.

Why are some identities and adjectives so hard for us to definitively claim? Why do we feel confident in claiming certain aspects of our identity but hesitant about others? What a fun question, right?

Look back to the Yes, No, Maybe So lists (page 50). Spend time with your maybes. Really sit with the words in your maybe column and reflect on why you do (or don't) feel comfortable owning those identities. Write down what you're thinking.

In a capitalist society, we are primed to believe that our primary identity is based on the work we get paid to do. When someone asks, "What do you do?" we tend to point to a title, a place of work, a paycheck, a business card, and the like to affirm our identity as a worker. I am a librarian. I work at a library. I went to school to learn how to do this work. I get paid to be a librarian. As far as identities go, this feels airtight—we have proof—which makes it a powerful mechanism for conflating and internalizing who we are with what we get paid to do.

Things get more complicated and less comfortable when we start exploring identities outside this fiscal proof. For example, you might write:

"Dancer. Artist. Writer.

"If I take dance classes as an adult for pure enjoyment, am I a dancer? I go to a studio every week, put on my tap shoes, and dance. I find joy in it. But am I a DANCER?

"I quilt. I have made dozens of elaborate quilts in my adult life. I have all the tools. I am in a quilt guild. But am I an ARTIST?

"I write every day. I have a blog and a small audience base. People read what I write. I love writing, and I am good at it. I haven't thus far made any money writing. Am I a WRITER?" What do you believe?

Of course you are a dancer, an artist, a writer! But, ultimately, it's up to you whether you feel like you can own those identities. What would it take to make you feel like you could authentically claim one of these identities? Why do you think there's so much tension around questions of identitiy? Where there is tension, there is an opportunity to explore and expand. Get curious about what these questions mean to you. Are you limiting yourself? Are you deferring to capitalist or patriarchal standards of who is allowed to hold certain identities? Do you feel like dabbling in something is not significant enough to claim it as an identity?

When you own an identity, you are far more likely to stay motivated to do the work to demonstrate it to yourself and others. Who is more likely to consistently show up for dance class, the person who declares themselves a dancer or the person who says they just take a dance class at the community center? Who is more likely to keep putting in the effort to ensure voting access for all, the person who identifies as a voting rights activist or the person who just writes some voter postcards and serves as a poll monitor?

Imagine what could be if we weren't afraid to claim all our identities. What do we lose in having more people claim the identity of artist, dancer, writer, or activist? Literally nothing.

everybody's got their something

THE PERFECT DAY

This activity offers a way to plan a future without the traditional trappings of capitalism. Rather than asking about goals, degrees, or career paths, it simply invites you to visualize and record what a perfect day in your life would be like . . . five years from now. It is an invitation to daydream with a focus on how you feel when you are living your perfect day. It's a way to explore your values and priorities and then reflect on where you currently stand in relationship to them. By clearly articulating the life you want, you can make choices that move you in that direction.

With intention, decision-making becomes less challenging. You simply ask, Does this decision serve my vision? You can see what needs to change and make choices to get you where you want to be and the kind of world you want to exist in.

Instructions: Imagine what your perfect day might be like in five years using the guiding questions below to gently steer you. Write the story of your perfect day in first person, as though it is happening or has happened—whatever flows most naturally for you as you write.

SOME GUIDING QUESTIONS

- How do you feel on your perfect day?
- What does the day look like?
- What do you do?
- Who do you spend your time with?
- What kind of people are you around?
- How much are you earning?
- How much are you giving?
- What do you fill your day with?
- What do you learn?
- What do you create?
- Who do you want to connect with?
- Where do you live?
- What does your house look like?
- What does it smell like?
- What do you do in the morning?
- What do you have for breakfast?

- What are you thinking about?
- Where do you spend the first half of the day?
- What do you have for lunch?
- Who do you eat with?
- Where do you eat?
- What are your friends like?
- What do you do for personal fulfillment?
- What life purpose are you striving toward?
- What is your business or job?
- What are your clients or coworkers like?
- What time do you start work?
- What do you actually do at work?
- What is your relationship like with your spouse? Family? Do you even have a partner? Do you have several?
- What do you talk about?
- Are you having sex? With whom?
- What is your intimacy like?
- What time do you go to bed?
- What do you think about when you go to bed?
- How do you sleep?

FOCUS ON THE "WHY" INSTEAD OF THE "WHAT"

WHAT	WHY
I have lots of money.	I have total financial freedom and am able to travel the world as I please.
I am the CEO of my company.	I am in a leadership position guiding my organization to success.
I live in a brownstone in Manhattan.	I have a safe, warm, and expansive home to live in where my family and friends love to gather.

IN SUMMARY

Write your life story in one sentence!

Don't be fooled by how simple this activity sounds—it is not easy! Our ego rebels against being summed up in so few words. Your sentence will reveal a lot about what identities and actions matter most to you.

Explore your activist identity.

Wikipedia defines activism in a way I really like: Activism consists of efforts to promote, impede, direct, or intervene in social, political, economic, or environmental reform with the desire to make changes in society toward a perceived greater good. Said differently, activism is effort and action to create positive change through reform. Is that something you do? Are you an activist?

What comes to mind when you hear the term *activist?* Maybe that word is too strongly attached to associations you have about what activism looks like. Do you picture marches, protests, strikes, violence, vandalism? Explore that. If you struggle to identify as an activist, perhaps it's because your definition of activism is limited or you hold judgment against the tactics other activists employ.

Is there a chance, however, that you might be downplaying all the work you actually are doing? I remember chatting with a woman who listed off at least 10 things she had done that month around abortion access. She had donated to an abortion fund and crocheted a piece for a craftivism project that drew attention to the issue. She had attended a training and was gearing up for her first day as a clinic escort. She was talking about it with friends, calling her elected officials, and sending out postcards to activate voters. I declared, "Wow! You are quite the activist these days, my friend." She immediately shut me down: "Oh, no. I'm not an activist. I just do what I can in my spare time." You see it, right?

Activism is not a competition. There is always someone doing more, and you know what those folks need? Support! Consider what skills you can lend to a person or group working in support of a cause you believe in. Are you a graphic designer? A spreadsheet ninja? Great at project management? A social media expert? Awesome at wrangling a crowd? Willing to show up when called upon? Just reaching out to ask "How can I help?" is taking action. More activists make the workload lighter and the impact more significant, and if more people thought of themselves as activists, there would be more people wielding the power of action.

And after all, that is what activism is. As my friend Omkari Williams always asks, "What if an activist looks like you?"

If you are finding that the term *activist* doesn't jibe as an identity you can own with confidence, perhaps you could try on some other words in the meantime? Change agent. Accomplice. Advocate. Champion. Reformer. Mutineer. Have fun exploring your identity!

An Activist by Any Other Name

There's power in the particular words we use to articulate our identities. A lot of people pause and struggle with identifying themselves as activists but appear more comfortable seeing themselves as craftivists. Craftivism has largely been positioned as an alternative form of activism, something quieter, gentler, more thoughtful. As a result, I see a lot of women, and white women in particular, easily slip into the identity of craftivist but still distance themselves from owning an activist identity. In some cases, I have seen direct language that positions craftivism in opposition to "megaphones and violence."

For women, "quiet and gentle" fits into the dominant narrative of how we are supposed to move through the world. Don't ruffle feathers or rock the boat. Don't get so emotional. Behave. Follow the rules. Smile. We are groomed to accept judgment and to shape our behaviors to stay within the lines and boundaries built by others to control us. Craftivism, as it is positioned now, provides a more comfortable and perhaps safer identity, especially for those who are already crafters and can point to material objects as proof of their craftivist efforts.

Craft is wildly valuable, but not all craft is craftivism. It is a big deal to call yourself an activist or a craftivist, because it does, in fact, demand that you take action on behalf of the issues that matter to you. Craftivism is not performance art.

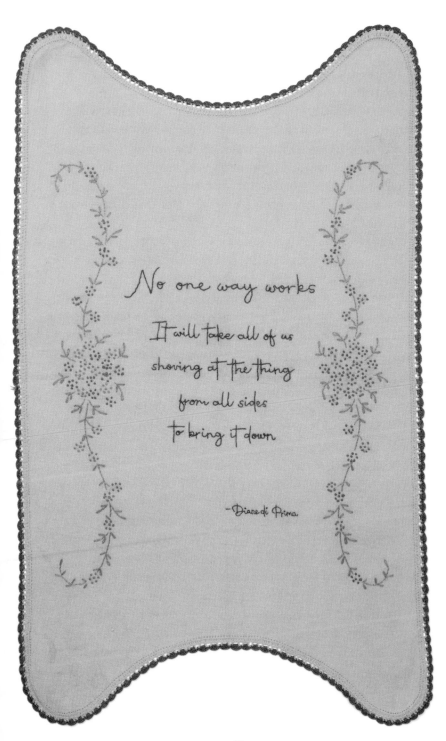

No one way works

It will take all of us
shoving at the thing
from all sides
to bring it down

—Diane di Prima

If you are a craftivist, you are an activist. Being an activist doesn't demand that you take to the streets with a megaphone. It doesn't demand anything of you except your commitment to take action around something that needs changing. Activism works best when it is a coordinated, multifaceted effort with myriad tactics serving the same goal, and that goal can be anything from protecting books from being banned in your local library to getting a candidate elected or ensuring that your neighbors are registered to vote and have a ride to the polls.

Craft can be a profound vehicle for so many tactics. I have used it to bring people into conversations on issues they would not normally engage with, like talking to young people about drugs, gun violence, accessibility, and trans rights. I've used it to gather diverse groups of thinkers to problem-solve and strategize domestic violence initiatives in their community and to formulate and uplift counternarratives around queer and feminist issues. I've used it to educate folks about issues and the different ways of taking action in service of those issues. Most important in all of these situations, craft has been a mechanism for bringing people together. Fostering relationships and community provides opportunities for individuals to grow their own impact as activists and empowers them to build in their community spaces. Craft has been the hook, but activism has always been the goal.

As mentioned at the beginning of this chapter, the only way to close the gap between your actions and your values is to dive deep into significant self-analysis. You need to ask yourself the hard questions in order to understand what you value, why you do what you do, and what stands in the way of taking action in service of the issues that matter to you. If you aren't willing to get uncomfortable and ask yourself these hard questions, you cannot be an effective activist.

I'm not a therapist, but I do know that sometimes all it takes is the right question at the right time from the right person to change everything. These are moments of impact. So, I'm going to throw some more things at you to consider. Stay curious, and have some fun with even more mildly uncomfortable self-reflection activities.

Let's get more uncomfortable.

I am a firm believer in embracing discomfort. You can expand your comfort zone by just agreeing to be uncomfortable.

The more you allow yourself to be in places, to have conversations, to do things that make you uncomfortable, the more comfortable you get with it. It's like magic. How does expanding your comfort zone make you a more effective activist? It makes you bolder and more confident speaking your truth and telling your story. When your comfort zone grows, you find the space to stretch out and live more authentically. Your fear is diminished. You are more powerful!

One reason I love to bring people together to craft and tackle difficult conversations is because crafting builds in a natural calm. It slows things down and gives folks an opportunity to move in and out of conversations at their pace and sit with uncomfortable feelings if they need to. (Let me also just add that feeling uncomfortable and feeling unsafe are two totally different things. I am in no way suggesting you should put yourself in unsafe situations. If an action or a conversation feels truly unsafe, don't do it.)

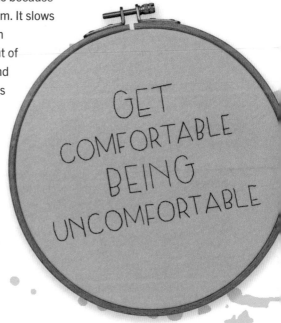

GET COMFORTABLE BEING UNCOMFORTABLE

CHALLENGING COMFORT

I once designed a project specifically to encourage folks to push beyond their comfort zones by participating in a street art campaign. I created a simple Martha Stewart–style tutorial for making your own wheatpaste to use as a glue. I produced dozens of posters that anyone could print from my website, and I invited people to go out and take a bit of a risk with unsanctioned art. It was a primer in breaking the rules, if you will.

I have truly loved hearing from people who have gone out pasting up these posters and the impact it had on them. No story was more powerful than the one I received from a group of activists in Cape Town, South Africa. After the brutal rape and murder of Uyinene Mrwetyana in a post office by a postal employee, there were massive protests against gender-based violence and femicide across the country. These activists printed out my posters and covered the walls of the post office as an act of resistance. #IAMNENE

Posters and tutorials can be found on my website to this day, should you feel like challenging yourself with a little street art adventure.

NOTICE & PRACTICE

The two keys to successfully growing your comfort zone are learning to notice when you are uncomfortable in a situation and then to practice staying present in that situation.

We have all heard of the "fight, flight, freeze, fawn" response. This automatic physiological reaction we have when our nervous system decides we are in danger is super useful when a bus is coming at us, but it's less helpful when it is triggered by someone asking us to think about our privileges. These moments demand that we override our code, recognize we are uncomfortable but not in danger, and stay present in that discomfort with curiosity.

Sometimes this is relatively easy. For example, if you are triggered by something in this book, you can mark the page, close the book, and have a think about what is making you uncomfortable. Other situations, like if you are eating dinner with friends and someone says something that feels triggering or challenging, can be more difficult to navigate. Here's my method for getting comfortable with being uncomfortable.

STEP I: NOTICE

When you notice a feeling of discomfort, pause, take a breath, and identify it. Say to yourself, out loud or internally, "I feel uncomfortable." Then spend a few moments exploring what you're feeling.

If you are in the middle of a conversation, give voice to your feelings and ask for a pause. You might say something along the lines of, "I'm having an emotional reaction to what you just said. I haven't quite figured out why, but it feels like it is butting up against a truth I hold, and I need to sit with it for a bit. Can we table this until I've done some more reflecting?" Alternatively, if you don't feel the need for a pause, you might ask, "Can we discuss this more so I can figure out what's up with me?"

STEP 2: PRACTICE

Once you've pinpointed the source of your discomfort, you have two options: You can dodge the discomfort and exist in the status quo, or you can confront the discomfort head-on and sit with it. Intentionally practicing being uncomfortable gradually expands your comfort zone as you slowly build up a tolerance to discomfort. If you are intentional and challenge yourself to do something each week that pushes your comfort zone, you'll be astounded by how quickly it works.

STEP 3: WORK IT

Does the idea of eating alone at a restaurant make you feel slightly uncomfortable? Take this book to a restaurant right now and eat by yourself. Notice how you feel. What are you thinking about? Are you wondering what other people are thinking about you? Do you feel lonely? What comes up for you?

Let's try a little something here. Make a list of things that make you uncomfortable, and then rank them from 1 (slightly uncomfortable) to 10 (somebody save me).

Now, go do one of these things! After you have done it, reflect on how it went and what you felt before, during, and after it, and consider how your feelings changed before, during, and after.

In case you're having a tough time coming up with ideas to challenge your comfort zone, I crowdsourced a few examples to help you get started:
- Addressing my uncle's racist comments at dinner
- Trying something new
- Publicly claiming an identity
- Sharing my thoughts on something deemed controversial
- Traveling by myself
- Wearing a bathing suit

- Asking for help
- Thinking about things that make me uncomfortable
- Not knowing exactly where I am going
- Being the only person of color in a roomful of people I don't know
- Being the only woman in a roomful of men
- Disappointing people
- Going back into the grocery store because I forgot something
- Asking younger people at work for help
- Speaking in a public setting
- Using coupons
- Attending an event where I don't know anyone
- Driving in a city
- Being outside in the dark

My Legacy

What is your legacy? What do you want your legacy to be? Write or make art about the legacy you want to leave behind.

My Obituary

This one is a little macabre, but we are embracing the discomfort, so let's dive in. Did you know that fewer than half of US adults have wills? It's true, and it's a supremely selfish decision not to have a will. We do such a great job avoiding all things related to our mortality that we foist the responsibility of dealing with everything we leave behind—including our bodies—onto our loved ones.

PROMPT: You can start dealing with some of the discomfort around death by writing your own obituary. What do you want people to know about you and your life after you are gone? Even if this exercise feels unsettling—and it probably will—try to have a little fun with it.

COFFEE & REFLECTION

Questions that inspire reflection provide us with low-stress opportunities to get to know ourselves better. We can explore our own thoughts and beliefs and journey back to their roots. We can probe how they may or may not serve us. A more nuanced understanding of self is a key element in our journey as activists.

PROMPTS FOR REFLECTION

- How do you feel about being a beginner at something?
- What would you say are your top three greatest skills?
- What do you appreciate most about yourself?
- What do you believe to be true about yourself?
- Who has influenced how you think about yourself?
- What is your personal mission statement?
- What do you value the most and the least in your relationships?
- When do you feel successful?
- When do you feel like you failed?
- What brings you the most joy?
- What words do other people use to describe you? Do you agree?
- When do you feel powerful?
- What are you afraid of?
- What do you remember about a time when you felt courageous?
- What do you find worthwhile in your work?
- What privileges do you hold?
- How has trauma impacted your personality and perspectives?
- When do you like to be in control? When do you like to relinquish it?
- How do your race, class, gender, age, faith, and geolocation impact how you move in the world and experience public spaces?

I enjoy choosing one prompt in the morning and thinking about it as I have my coffee. I find that if I practice this reflection in the morning, it sort of pops up throughout the day as well. You could journal some of these. Use them as prompts for your making practice. Use them as conversation starters with friends. No rules. Just tools!

MAKE ART ABOUT YOURSELF

Take all the things you have been reflecting on about yourself and your lived experiences and turn them into a piece of art—whatever you like. Use the reflection questions from Coffee & Reflection as prompts.

Make art that centers you. Then reflect on your process and outcomes.

- What did you focus on?
- What did you leave out?
- What did you learn?

- What do you want to change for your future?

The process of making and reflecting has a great deal to teach us about how we think about ourselves.

BADASS HERSTORY

The idea for my ongoing project Badass Herstory came about when I realized just how few of the women I was interacting with personally and professionally make art for themselves, let alone about themselves. The collection has grown to hundreds of 12-inch by 12-inch pieces of fiber art through which women, femmes, and nonbinary folks share their stories. What I continue to learn and hear from participants is that it is a profoundly challenging and deeply transformative experience to create art about yourself. There is power in owning your story and freedom in sharing it through art. You are, of course, invited to participate in Badass Herstory. All of the details can be found on my website.

I REALLY DO CARE

This activity is going to drive a lot of our action throughout the rest of the book. You will be honing your efforts and learning to build out strategies. Knowing where you want to focus your efforts is critical to the work we are going to do together. If you do only one activity, do this one.

Make a list of 10 issues you care about that you feel you must take action on.

Examples: voting access, abortion rights, houselessness, animal rights, green energy, prison abolition, defunding the police, pay equity, universal health care, racial equality, immigration and refugee rights, gun violence, food insecurity, disability rights, queer rights, genocide, war, substance abuse, human trafficking, end-of-life reform, labor rights, student loans, economic justice, decriminalizing sex work, church sex abuse . . . to name a few.

What are you already doing that is relevant to these issues?

Which of the issues do you want to be doing more about?

Now—and this is going to be uncomfortable—circle the three issues you would prioritize as the most important to you. No one is going to judge you. They are all important, but you must pick three. I love you. You can do this.

Congratulations, my friend.

You made it through the gauntlet of uncomfortable things. Remember, the journey of being human is a never-ending journey, and this chapter is meant to jump-start your brain into thinking in new directions and seeing question marks everywhere. Try these activities at a pace that works for you, revisit them as you work your way through the book, and come back anytime you want to have some uncomfortable fun. Most importantly, stay open and curious, and question everything. Let's start to reimagine what is possible in this world and within ourselves!

NO
HUMAN
BEING
IS
ILLEGAL

Quote by Elie Wiesel

CHAPTER 3

'CAUSE WE DON'T KNOW IT ALL

RESEARCH

After completing the I Really Do Care activity (page 72), you should have a list of three issues you are committed to exploring further. As you make your way through this book, you will be able to narrow it down to one. We're working toward zeroing in on one core issue to ensure you can create an activism strategy that is built on a foundation of proactive, consistent, and manageable action (while also making sure you're not heading down the road to burnout). Committing your energy, attention, and focus to the issue that is most meaningful to you will allow you to really dive deep, which is vital to achieving and maintaining material change.

While staying focused on a core issue is important, sometimes we need to redirect our efforts to support other activists during times of crisis. When leaders in the United States started putting children in cages at the border between the US and Mexico, millions of people and organizations put everything else aside to concentrate their efforts on ending this horrific crime against humanity. It was an immediate and pressing need that demanded a redistribution of energy and action, and activists around the world showed up in solidarity.

In order to help solve a problem, you need to have a deep, thorough understanding of the issues contributing to that problem. Issues of injustice are all intertwined, and you may find that your path shifts or your focus narrows as you start to identify the intersections where you feel you can have the most impact. That's a good thing! Follow the path and see where it leads you. We must work on all paths to unravel the whole mess, but focusing your efforts doesn't mean you aren't having an impact in other areas. Pull the strings you can pull, and trust that others are pulling theirs.

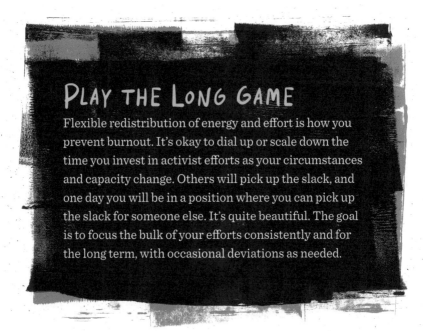

PLAY THE LONG GAME

Flexible redistribution of energy and effort is how you prevent burnout. It's okay to dial up or scale down the time you invest in activist efforts as your circumstances and capacity change. Others will pick up the slack, and one day you will be in a position where you can pick up the slack for someone else. It's quite beautiful. The goal is to focus the bulk of your efforts consistently and for the long term, with occasional deviations as needed.

Go down the rabbit hole as you start to research an issue, explore all the avenues, and learn everything you can. Even though you're working to build a deep knowledge base, free yourself from the idea that you have to tackle every injustice you come across during your research. It's impossible to do everything, but as you work through the steps outlined here, you will gradually find the path of action that's best suited to you—your beliefs, abilities, skill sets, and the time you have to devote to sustained action.

Ready to take that first step? Start by choosing one of your three issues, and prepare to consume and listen.

Consume

Start by consuming a lot of media—books, articles, documentaries, television shows, movies, podcasts, blogs. Look for art, music, and events that relate to the issue you're interested in exploring. It's about getting as much information as possible from as many perspectives as possible, including viewpoints that you believe are on the wrong side of history. It's important to understand all of the arguments and narratives, even when they don't seem to make sense or you feel in your gut that they're abjectly wrong.

Do research into the history of the issue to see how it has changed or evolved. Can you get to a place where you understand the evolution of the issue you're interested in and the key players involved over time, what their motivations were, and the impact their work has had on the issue?

Listen

A copious amount of listening is pivotal when immersing yourself in the culture around your chosen issue. Find folks who are in the space already, and listen to what they are saying. Follow social media accounts and attend virtual and in-person events. Listening—ears open, mouth shut—helps you expand your understanding and identify any important variations in approach or philosophy among those already in the movement. This can help you delineate your own position on the issue and clarify who you feel most in alignment with.

For example, on the abortion front, I choose to align with activists who encourage pro-abortion messaging versus pro-choice messaging. While we are all working toward the same goal, the former aligns better with how I want the conversation around abortion framed because I feel strongly that destigmatizing the word *abortion* is important to progress and to alleviating societal-induced shame. I've done a lot of listening in this space, and I hear quite often from people who feel that *pro-choice* is a "gentler" and more palatable counternarrative to *pro-life*. I understand that angle, but I disagree with it. I believe abortion is health care, and I am in favor of everyone having access to the health care they need. Just as I don't believe we need gentler narratives when we talk about heart transplants or dialysis, I also don't believe we need a gentler narrative about abortion access. That said, I certainly hold no judgment of those who align with pro-choice messaging, as we are allies with different perspectives working for a similar outcome.

Understanding and clarifying what my beliefs are through a lot of listening and learning has allowed me to zero in on the intersection of this complicated issue that is aligned with my vision and where I center my activist energies.

It's on you.

Educating yourself on issues that are new to you is wholly your responsibility. If you are in a position of privilege (racial, socioeconomic, gender, sexuality, ability, etc.), do not make it the responsibility of those who have been marginalized to educate you. As a queer person who has been out for more than 25 years, I have been asked innumerable triggering and inappropriate questions by strangers who wanted to be considered allies. Seemingly well-meaning queries like "Are you sure?" (usually followed by "You don't look gay") or "Is your family

PRO APPENDECTOMY

PRO ORGAN TRANSPLANT

PRO DIALYSIS

PRO VACCINE

PRO JOINT REPLACEMENT

PRO INSULIN

PRO STENT

PRO ABORTION

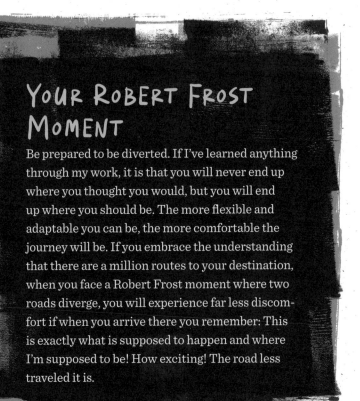

Your Robert Frost Moment

Be prepared to be diverted. If I've learned anything through my work, it is that you will never end up where you thought you would, but you will end up where you should be. The more flexible and adaptable you can be, the more comfortable the journey will be. If you embrace the understanding that there are a million routes to your destination, when you face a Robert Frost moment where two roads diverge, you will experience far less discomfort if when you arrive there you remember: This is exactly what is supposed to happen and where I'm supposed to be! How exciting! The road less traveled it is.

disappointed?" or "So you don't like guys?" do actual harm. Some are so deeply steeped in heteronormative thinking—"But who is the man in the relationship?"—that I find it impossible to even respond.

Consume and listen. When you connect with the message or style of a content creator, start to dig into their connections. Whose content do they share? Who do they stand in opposition to? Keep diving. If you find someone whose media is particularly helpful and you lean on their content quite a bit, drop them some cash and a thank-you. Gradually you will accumulate enough baseline knowledge and connect organically with people in a way in which asking questions will be a welcome part of a reciprocal exchange of ideas. That's the goal. First prove you are committed to learning and conspiring with those who have been marginalized.

Narrow

You've consumed, listened, and been mindful of how you're educating yourself on the core issues you identified. What do you do with all the knowledge you've accumulated so far? How do you find your point of entry? Working in your own community is a great jumping-off place. When you start local, you can develop a nuanced understanding of how an issue directly impacts your neighbors and your neighborhood. Instead of being an overwhelming proposition, the work becomes a collaborative community effort that can grow and expand.

Let's say immigration rights are one of the issues you want to focus on. Excellent. Where to start? Here's a true story from Chicago.

Case Study: #ProtectRP

Chicago is a city of neighborhoods, each with its own totally unique vibe. It is also a sanctuary city, which means that city officials will not ask anyone about their immigration status, disclose that information to authorities, or, most importantly, deny anyone city services based on their immigration status. Rogers Park, on the far northeast side of the city, is one of the most diverse neighborhoods in Chicago, with more than 40 languages spoken within a 1.84-square-mile radius and a large immigrant and refugee population. When President Trump won the presidency in 2016 on a platform that included strong anti-immigration campaign promises, the threat of deportations in Chicago suddenly became very real. Rogers Park neighbors came together and created a neighborhood movement called #ProtectRP. Folks with various skill sets came forward and started organizing community meetings, Know Your Rights workshops, and other initiatives.

Perhaps most impressively, in response to talk of targeted immigration raids by ICE (the US Immigration and Customs Enforcement agency), a group of community members developed a training curriculum to prepare neighbors for standoffs with government officials. The resistance trainings were open to all community members and were designed to prepare them to show up to ICE raids and witness, document, and interrupt. There was a phone tree and volunteers whose job was to show up to homes and businesses when a report came in to verify that an ICE raid was actually happening. This would trigger mobilization of the #ProtectRP network—anyone who was trained and able would show up to the location to bear witness, document what was happening, and interrupt the raid. All of this was planned, organized, and executed by individuals in the community. Statewide, advocacy organizations were simultaneously working hard to move forward the TRUST Act (ultimately adopted in 2017), which prohibited police from working with ICE and prevented them from detaining and arresting anyone based on their immigration status. #ProtectRP has become an important model of how hyperlocal organized community action can transform a neighborhood and protect lives. Starting where you live is the fastest way to create visible and radical change. Especially when it feels like an issue is too big and insurmountable.

It was a marvel to witness and be a small part of #ProtectRP. It felt like everyone in the city was working in concert—from the people who donated space for community trainings to the legislation—to protect our most vulnerable community members. Every single action mattered. And all those actions were supported with art and through craft. Stickers and signs covered Rogers Park, declaring intentions and providing resources. Zines and other well-designed educational materials were crucial to ensuring that folks understood their rights and had access to important phone numbers and email addresses. As you read this little case study, I am certain you've thought of 10,000 ways in which craft and art could have supported this work. Creative minds are vital to social and political change.

Support

Once you feel like you have found your people within a movement, you can look for opportunities to connect, uplift, amplify, and support. That can range from retweeting them to attending their events to creating a piece of art to draw attention to their work.

When creating art as a mechanism for amplifying another activist's work, reach out to them first to get permission and to make sure they're on board with how you plan to show your support. Be sure to compensate them for any time they spend working with you on the content development, whether that is a direct payment, a donation to their organization, or gifting them the art piece. I've seen too many instances where the people whose work is being uplifted are not consulted in advance or are otherwise left out of a well-meaning amplification initiative, and it can inadvertently lead to harm. Consider the case of the social media blackout to support Black Lives Matter in June 2020. While it was likely a well-intentioned action on the part of those who started it, the blackout, in which people took over the #BlackLivesMatter hashtag and posted black boxes in their profiles, ran counter to the desires and strategies of the Black Lives Matter movement. The movement relied upon that hashtag to share vital information and resources in real time. By taking it over, supporters essentially blinded the movement for several days at a critical moment.

At this stage in your process, a solid move is to find ways to support the others who are doing work that aligns with your beliefs, without any expectation that they will take on additional labor in order to help you help them. As an example, after the US Supreme Court overturned *Roe v. Wade* in 2022, ending the constitutional right to abortion, millions of people were desperate to do something. This in itself was a wonderful thing. However, abortion providers and organizations like Planned Parenthood, NARAL, and the National Network of Abortion Funds that have been leading this work for decades (and warning us this was coming for years) were inundated and overwhelmed by requests and demands for ways people could help. In my own Facebook feed, an acquaintance railed about her attempts to volunteer at a local abortion clinic. She was furious that she hadn't received a call back in two days. She was looking to self-soothe through volunteerism and was angry that her needs were not being met, but she was also oblivious to how disruptive the groundswell of well-intentioned outreach was to the day-to-day operation of the local clinic.

I felt helpless and defeated by the ruling, and, like so many others, I donated money. But I wanted to do more. For years I had been following the work Abortion Access Front did in supporting abortion funds across the country as well as bringing attention to forced-birthers (a.k.a. pro-lifers), and I thoroughly enjoyed their funny, sassy, pro-abortion messaging on social media. Immediately after the Supreme Court decision, they launched a daylong training to help people better understand the support needed to ensure that pregnant people can access affirming abortion care. I attended the training and promoted it across all my digital platforms to ensure my community knew about this amazing resource. After the training, I reached out to the organization's director of development with an idea I thought might be helpful: I wanted to support Abortion Access Front in developing more consistent donors over the next year.

For nonprofits, recurring monthly donors are hugely important. When a movement experiences a critical blow (like the fall of *Roe v. Wade*), organizations are often immediately inundated with donations. While a massive influx of money is fantastic and goes a long way, those donations dry up over time as we normalize new realities or another issue finds itself in the spotlight. The unpredictable ebb and flow of donations makes it very challenging for nonprofits to plan, project, and sustain the work they do, which is why consistent donors are essential.

I made it clear in my initial email to the director of development that I would take on the bulk of the labor. Then, with the organization's approval, I created an initiative I like to think of as a craft-of-the-month club to fund abortion access. I recruited 11 other craftivists who worked in a variety of mediums, including knitting, quilting, crochet, embroidery, zine making, sewing, and cross-stitching. I pulled together a schedule and began managing the project in collaboration with Abortion Access Front. Each month, one of the craftivists created a relevant craft pattern, and the collective promoted the pattern to their digital communities. Anyone who donated more than $10 to the organization received a free download of the pattern. The fundraiser ran from November 2022 to December 2023 and raised thousands of dollars.

The takeaway here is that I saw a clear need and an opportunity to use my knowledge base, skill sets, and networks to help. During this moment of crisis, I reached out to Abortion Access Front with an idea and a tangible plan that I could execute to support their organization. In doing so, I was able to help while not adding much burden or additional work to their already overloaded staff.

"How can I help?" is a fantastic question in routine times. "Here's how I believe I can help" is more useful in moments of crisis. There are a million ways to support issue and movement leaders. Lean into your skill sets, your networks, and the ideas that bubble up!

Engage

My friend, you are ready! It's time to get in there and engage! You have gained knowledge by voraciously consuming media and listened to various voices and perspectives around an issue to understand the landscape. You know who is working in the space in a way that you align with and have connected with a

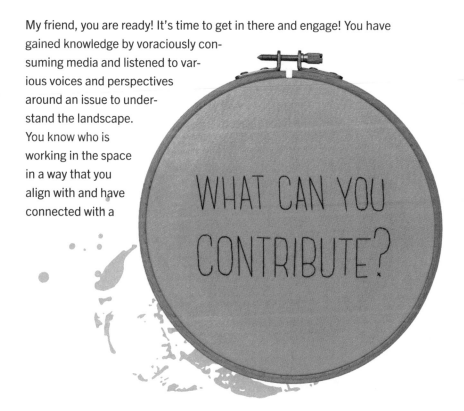

WHAT CAN YOU CONTRIBUTE?

diverse cross section of community members. I can all but guarantee that you have loads of ideas for how to draw from your knowledge base, your unique lived experiences, and your skill sets to contribute to the initiatives that align with your beliefs. I'm willing to bet most of them will be wicked crafty! You should feel confident offering them up and moving them forward.

Creative Ways to Engage

The easiest way to engage with activism is to volunteer or otherwise be of service to people and organizations you have connected with who inspire you and light you up. There are endless ways to use your time, talents, and networks to lend support.

- Are you a connector? The person who seems to know everyone? Help your favorite nonprofit recruit board members!

- Are you an athlete or aspiring athlete? Turn your next competition into a fundraising moment.

- Birthday coming up? Have a party, and ask guests to skip the gift and instead bring new underwear, socks, and period supplies to donate to your local shelter.

- Are you handy? Follow the example of some rad folks in Chicago who host a free community repair clinic each month.

- Does your company have a corporate match policy? You can double your donation with one form!

- Watching too much Marie Kondo? Partner up with your neighbors and host a massive yard sale to raise funds for your local mutual aid group.

- Like to bake? Who doesn't love a good old-fashioned bake sale? Bake Sale for Abortion Funds has a nice ring to it.

Activism can look any way you want it to. Get creative and flex your skills!

Quote by Daniel Pink

Know Your Role

It's important to explore the various roles you can play in support of the issues you want to invest your time and energy in, and then pause to carefully consider what the most appropriate role for you might be. Oh, did you think you were done with self-reflection? Surprise! It never ends.

Here are a few questions to start with:

- Are you directly impacted by this issue?
- Are you in a position of privilege and hope to leverage that privilege in support of the issue?
- Should you be in a leadership position?
- Should your work be in support of leaders?

Many great thinkers, including Deepa Iyer and Omkari Williams, have done amazing work to help make self-reflection in this context easier by offering well-articulated guidance on what roles are necessary to ensure that a movement progresses. I am particularly drawn to how Deepa Iyer frames the many roles that exist within the social change ecosystem. The roles defined below are from her 2019 article for Medium (online) titled "My Role in a Social Change Ecosystem: A Mid-Year Check-In," and it's well worth seeking out more of Deepa's work.

Here are some categories to think about:

FRONTLINE RESPONDERS quickly and ably transition into rapid-response mode and organize resources, networks, and messages.

HEALERS tend to the individual and intergenerational traumas of white supremacy, racism, colonialism, capitalism, patriarchy, and nativism.

STORYTELLERS AND ARTISTS bind the past and present, channeling the histories and experiences of our ancestors to shed light on what is possible today.

BRIDGE BUILDERS can work across divisions with patience and compassion.

DISRUPTORS speak up and take action, especially when doing so is uncomfortable and risky.

CAREGIVERS provide nourishment to organizers, exude concern and love, and create a community of care.

VISIONARIES have the ability to find, articulate, and reconnect us to our north star, even when we cannot clearly see the sky.

BUILDERS actively develop the ideas, structures, and scaffolding for our organizations and movements.

Do you see yourself in one of those roles? Perhaps in many of those roles? Our roles may change based on our skills, limitations, privileges, and timing, but every role is needed and valuable.

Finding Your Activist Archetype

In her book *Micro Activism*, Omkari Williams identifies different activist archetypes to help us clarify what roles we might play within a movement.

> **THE PRODUCER** holds the image of the big picture so that others can play their essential roles. Their biggest driver is accomplishing the communities' larger goals, and they are most comfortable in a supporting role.
>
> **THE INDISPENSABLE** takes a behind-the-scenes role, working down in the trenches doing the unglamorous work of the everyday.
>
> **THE HEADLINER** is a leader who is happy to stand in the spotlight, so long as it serves the big vision.
>
> **THE ORGANIZER** loves to use their organizing skills to put together detailed plans of action toward achieving goals.

There are so many roles that need to be filled within a movement—there really is a place for everyone! Every role is vital, and each person who becomes involved brings with them their unique strengths, temperaments, and current circumstances. While we are united in showing up to support a common cause we believe in, each person brings diverse perspectives and lived experiences to the table.

Let's say you live in a state that has recently passed legislation restricting drag performances in public spaces. You and your community are outraged about this and other anti-LGBTQ+ legislation appearing in your state and across the country. You decide to organize a drag story hour to bring attention to the issue, to stand in protest, and to mobilize community. You are a frontline responder. You recognized a need for responsive action, and you are leading the charge. (Well done, you!)

You reach out to the builders whose work aligns with the issue. You call in your queer and allied friends and the local drag community, and you reach out to LGBTQ+ advocacy organizations, the feminist bookstore, the neighborhood pride group, and the LGBTQ+ chamber of

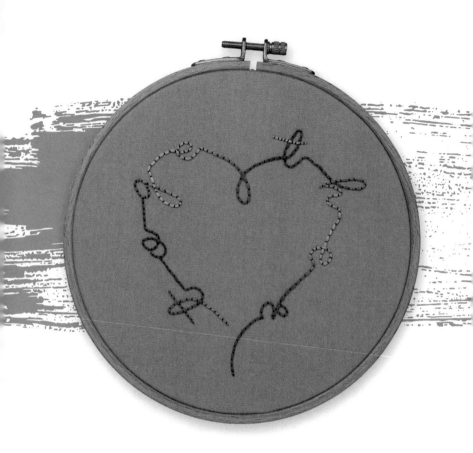

commerce. You invite everyone to a planning meeting where the builders will work to ensure that the strategy, talking points, and PR for the event align with the initiatives and campaigns the group is working on.

Several of the drag performers stand out as inspiring leaders who inject the meeting with hope and humor, always reminding the group of what is possible and what is beautiful. These visionaries ensure that the beauty and possibility shape the strategy.

The group identifies disruptors who will interface with the press ahead of and during the event.

Drag performers volunteer to take the stage and lead the stories. Other queer storytellers and artists create promotional materials, everything from digital collateral to posters, which they post in public spaces around town. They take to social media to flood the airways with rich stories and art that spread the word about the legislation, the event, and other actions viewers can take. They create a relevant art-making activity to engage youth participants at the storytelling event.

Caregivers are entrusted with welcoming and directing guests as well as arranging for beverages and snacks. Another group of caregivers serve as security through a visible and significant presence in front of the bookstore.

The event is kicked off by a queer historian who provides a powerful anecdote reminding everyone of the resiliency and progress of the queer community despite generations of oppression. This healer holds perspective and inspires hope.

Several bridge builders stand outside, ready to engage with curious passersby as well as any potential counterprotestors. The advocacy organizations have reached out to elected officials and power holders to invite them to the story hour.

Where would you see yourself in this example? Are you able to identify roles that would be a good fit? A bad fit?

That was invigorating!

It is quite a magical journey from "I want to help" to "I am informed, self-aware, and helping," but you are committed to the long game as a lifelong activist. By choosing one issue to focus on and learning as much as you can by reading, watching, and listening, you develop a shrewd understanding of that issue. This rigorous and continuous inquiry enables you to refine your own perspectives and opinions. The more nuanced your understanding of an issue, the easier it is to identify opportunities for change and the role you can take in making that change happen. But the trip down the rabbit hole isn't over yet. Now we need to get to the root of the problem!

CHAPTER 4

GETTING TO THE ROOTS

IDENTIFY AND DEFINE THE PROBLEMS

A few years back I was in a meeting when I heard someone casually ask if this was a baby-in-the-river moment. Several people in the room laughed and nodded. I felt like I was in an episode of *The Office*. I looked to the imaginary camera and gave it my best WTH face. I'm sort of known for my WTH faces, so it triggered an explanation.

The story of babies in the river:

We are standing by a riverbank, and we see a baby float by. Holy shit! There's a baby in the river. We rush into the water to save it. A second baby floats by. Zoinks! Another baby. More and more babies float down the river. We get volunteers. We set up a medical tent. We get formula and blankets and spend our time rescuing the babies. At what point do we send a team upriver to find out where the heck the babies are coming from?

It's an odd little analogy for the idea that we will never be able to truly solve a problem (in this case, babies floating down a river) if we don't seek out and identify the cause of the problem. We will always just be treating the symptoms.

Getting to the root of any problem can be incredibly challenging because often many factors are in play, and usually there are several root causes for any issue. Additionally, we can't ignore the symptoms while we work on solving the root cause. Imagine if we just let the babies float on by and drown while we went upstream to figure out why they were there and who was chucking them in the river in the first place! We must do both.

The thing is, identifying the root cause of a problem doesn't necessarily mean you can resolve it. Sometimes it takes years, decades, or even lifetimes to do that. No need to despair. When you can see a problem—no matter how big—you can start to work on it. This is what deconstructing systems looks like. It's seeing the big picture, naming it, showing it to everyone, and then taking action to treat the symptoms *and* work on the solutions that will eventually eradicate the source of the problem.

Take Galileo. Galileo identified a measurement problem: We have no idea how fast light travels. He did not solve this problem; he simply identified it as something that could not be solved at present but, when solved, might help us answer some pressing questions. Good on you, Galileo. Sorry the Roman Catholic Church locked you up as a heretic for your wild claim that Earth is not the center of the universe.

Here's the thing: He identified a problem in the early 1600s, and other scientists worked on it until 1983! In that year, an international commission on weights and measures set the speed of light at 299,792,458 meters per second (that's 186,282 miles per second for us anti-metric Americans). And now it's up to today's scientists to use that math to invent warp drive so I can live out my Star Trek captain fantasies. I'm certain that's what Galileo intended.

We are our own worst enemy.

Most problems are a complex amalgam of issues that I like to categorize as follows: human factors, physical factors, and organizational/systemic factors.

Humans, everything we touch—am I right?—cause all sorts of problems usually by doing or not doing something. This doing or not doing can often lead to physical problems. This is when tangible stuff fails. This doing or not doing can also lead to organizational problems. Mostly it comes back to us humans as the root of our own problems. The upside is that we can solve these problems if we really want to. We have so much potential.

Let's look at an example. Some humans said, "You know what we need? An easier way to make individual cups of coffee at the office. Making pots of coffee throughout the day leads to coffee waste, deep frustration, and confusion: How old is that coffee? Who left the coffee pot empty again? Is this really decaf?" The office coffee problem is endless.

Along comes Keurig.

In the early 1990s, humans John Sylvan and Peter Dragone invented the single-cup brewing system. Ooooh, baby! Now it's every coffee drinker for themselves. No more communal coffee nonsense. You want coffee? Go pop a K-Cup into the machine and brew it yourself.

Fast-forward a few years, and more than nine *billion* K-Cups have been sold. Nine billion plastic and aluminum K-Cups. Nine billion non-recyclable and nonbiodegradable K-Cups. That certainly throws some weight behind our global plastics problem, eh? So we have identified a massive global plastics problem, and we know that our plastic waste is literally killing our oceans. No oceans, no humans. Interesting. In our desire to stick it to the people we share workspace with, we invent a product that creates massive amounts of plastic waste.

Then the single-cup brewing system patent expires, and it's a mad capitalist race to get a cut of the single-cup market. More waste. Some humans pause and say, "Hey! This seems to be creating a lot of waste." Other humans amplify that message. People get uncomfortable. We see the problem, but the K-Cups are so convenient, and we are used to them now. Going back to the pot would be madness. Additionally some people are making a shit ton of money off these products. So we attempt to treat a few of the symptoms by reengineering some of the cups. Let's find a way to make the cups biodegradable or reusable. Let's try this and let's try that.

This stunner was made by my dad, Martin Downey, whom I taught to stitch at the age of 70. He worked it using a pattern by @BloomandFloss.

We know that we can simply eliminate these plastics from the equation. We can just stop. We stop making them. We stop using them. We go back to the good old-fashioned pot of coffee. But we won't, because in 20 years the K-Cup has become part of our culture. We are stubborn.

It's simple and wildly complex. We are so quick to adopt what is easy or what serves us as humans, with such little analysis. We are slow to sacrifice convenience and comfort for what is healthy and in our best interests. The desire to change is made exponentially weaker for those who could eradicate the problem when they are making billions of dollars off their creation. Change becomes even more challenging when the harmful convenient stuff is the only thing that vast majorities of the population can afford. We literally prevent folks from being able to make more thoughtful choices.

There we have it. Humans creating solutions that create problems that add to other problems we have created. See why it can be so challenging?

As a side note, John Sylvan has said that sometimes he feels bad that he ever invented the single-cup brewing system. I hope that is a big reminder to designers and inventors that human-centered design thinking is no longer sufficient.

I got 99 problems.

Identifying the cause of a problem is the first step in fixing it. So how do we identify problems? Most of the time, we identify a problem easily when it impacts us personally. When we feel discomfort or annoyance, we can point to the thing causing it and declare that thing a problem. When someone else shares with us a problem they have identified, we are far more likely to take interest if we, too, have experienced this problem. Perhaps we didn't even know it was a problem until someone else named it for us. Other times, we hear people point out a problem they have, but we have never experienced such a problem. We ask, "Is that a real problem? Is it their problem? Does it have to also be my problem?" All are valid experiences and questions.

Fun fact: I am wildly undiscerning in my consumption of television. I was recently watching a docuseries called *The Queen of Versailles*, in which the matriarch of a family with billions of dollars is leading the charge to finish building the country's largest private home near Orlando, Florida. I watched, mouth agape, at what for me was a horrific display of greed and hoarding. I also watched with fascination as this woman and her family expressed their very real anxiety and stress at learning they would not be able to purchase and keep flamingos on their property due to licensing and laws protecting these birds. To them, this was a real problem. Those around them decided this was not their problem, and so there would be no flamingos. Don't worry, they got toucans instead. (They matched the furniture better, anyway).

Perspective is important in the process of identifying problems, especially when we wish to involve others in addressing them.

IF I WERE GIVEN ONE HOUR
TO SAVE THE PLANET,
I WOULD SPEND 59 MINUTES
DEFINING THE PROBLEM AND
ONE MINUTE RESOLVING IT.

— ALBERT EINSTEIN

A Formula

Being an activist is being a problem solver. That doesn't mean spending your life looking for problems. It can mean being joyfully curious about our world, asking questions about why things are the way they are, and looking for ways to make life a little easier for everyone. What does that look like? We can break it down into (ta-da!) a five-step formula:

1. Observe
2. Listen
3. Wonder
4. Believe others
5. Confront reality

Observe

Observation is a brilliant teacher. It allows us to identify patterns. Patterns are endlessly helpful in identifying things that need to change. We are all voyeurs to some extent. Reality TV and social media would not exist if we weren't. We can channel that trait into something a bit more refined. Think of it more as radical curiosity. Everyone is capable of radical curiosity with a little practice. The more you can stand in a space of curiosity, the more curious you become. It's like love, hope, gratitude, and creativity. You can never run out, and it grows exponentially with attention and focus.

Can you see the world with fresh eyes every day? Wonder about why things are the way they are? Can you marvel at the mundane? See people as magical beings and simply observe their adorable and confounding quirks and behaviors? Of course you can. It's a practice, and it requires intention. The next time you go to the grocery store, enter it as though you have never been in a grocery store before. Watch how humans behave. Marvel at the incredible and vast selection of foods available to you. Think about the people involved in getting a pear from a tree to you. Shopping carts! What an incredible invention. Who thought of that? See what I mean?

Listen

Falling in tandem with observing is listening. Sometimes it looks like eavesdropping—listening to all the conversations happening around you. Sometimes it looks like scrolling—social media makes it incredibly easy to listen to people from all over the world at any moment. It is such a gift to have access to so many thoughts and lived experiences.

Once I brought students into the exhibits at a local art museum. I asked them to think about their creative process. Where do they get inspiration from? I gave them blindfolds and invited them to sit in the exhibits with their blindfolds on and listen. They seemed to find this cool but counterintuitive. Most art is meant to be looked at, after all. What happens if you listen to art? What will you feel and learn if you experience an art museum by listening to how other people experience the art? Is there information and inspiration to be gained? Listen and marvel at what you really hear.

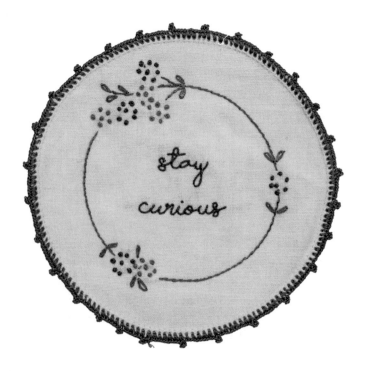

Wonder

Wondering is time spent just thinking, letting your mind go where it wants. There is great overlap between being an activist and being an artist, and it lies in this experience of wonder, curiosity, contemplation, and thinking. It is the experience of developing a creative process. Wonder is key to identifying patterns. It cracks open the potential for reimagining what could be. We need creative minds to see through the fog and envision our communities, societies, and world as they could be.

My wondering time is usually spent walking and staring (not in a creepy way). I take walks around my neighborhood, in the woods, on the beach, or on my treadmill if the weather isn't cooperating. I leave my earbuds at home, and I let my mind run buck wild. I don't judge a single thought. If I spot something interesting, I stop and spend time staring at it. I'm particularly drawn to flowers, interesting tree bark, and signs. I like to bring a notebook, as I usually come up with my best ideas when I wander and wonder.

If you're particularly stressed, a wonder walk can quickly turn into an anxiety walk. The mind naturally wanders to all the things we are worried about. Wondering is something to practice with intention, just like observing. On days when you're having trouble keeping your mind centered in wonder, try coming up with a juicy question and focusing your wonder on that. It almost always works.

Acknowledge and Believe

We humans really like to live in the space where something that isn't a problem for us just isn't a problem at all. If it doesn't directly impact us, then it's someone else's problem, and either they are lying about having a problem or it's theirs to deal with.

But we must be willing to believe others. This links back to curiosity and is deeply entwined with empathy. We don't need to make every problem our own, but we also should not invalidate the experiences of others. When we listen and believe others and stay curious about their experiences and thoughts, our eyes are opened. This clarity expands empathy and can often illuminate our blind spots.

CHANNEL YOUR INNER VULCAN

The date is April 5, 2063. The location is Bozeman, Montana. You are an alien species, and you just made first contact with humanity. You spend a day watching these humans. As you observe and eavesdrop on them in their daily lives, what do you learn? What questions arise as you wonder about what you are seeing and hearing? When you speak to them (using your universal translator), what do they tell you about their lives and culture? Does that align with what you notice? What do these observations lead you to believe about humans? Use your senses. Look for patterns. Can you see humanity through a new lens?

Confront Reality

We must confront reality. Isn't it funny that this must be said? Humans are amazing at magical thinking. I get it. Sometimes ignorance really is bliss, or at least a shield to protect us from the hard truths. But you are reading this book, which means you are not the kind of person who is content to live like that. You take the red pill. You face what is, so that you can create what could be. Activists are always looking for places and spaces that could benefit from change. We are part sleuth and part seer. Activism invites us to detach from what we think we know and examine everything with radical curiosity.

A Case Study in Identifying a Problem

In December 2020, I observed a trend within my community. I was hearing a lot of folks talk about how excited they were for 2021. There was a real energetic focus on the transition out of 2020 and into a new year that was certainly going to be better than what 2020 had delivered (a global pandemic and profound social unrest). I love new-year energy. I was worried about this particular brand.

I started listening harder and asking questions. The problem I was seeing was blind enthusiasm for an event that would yield no significant impact on our lived experience. Nothing was going to change simply because the calendar flipped from 2020 to 2021. I was concerned about the impact that would have on the mental health and motivation of folks who were focusing on 2021 as a solution for the shit show that was our current lives.

I felt like I needed to intervene. I observed and listened more. I uncovered a few things.

1. People feel motivated to change around New Year's. This is not a new or surprising discovery, but this year felt different. People seemed to be expecting *gestures broadly* *things to change* but didn't seem as focused on *their* change.

2. The great long horror of 2020 had two opposite impacts on creativity: Either folks dove into their creative practice with fury or they lost all capacity for creativity.

We know that being creative and analog-making (making things by hand) positively impacts our mental health and well-being. I wondered whether it was possible to channel the new-year hopefulness and motivation into an opportunity to support people through the transition, setting them up for success in the coming year.

I decided to name the problem I was seeing. I just put it out there that I was worried that folks were so enthusiastic about the new year—and I could see the enthusiasm hangover hitting fast and hard. Next, I invited everyone to channel that energy into using January 2021 to develop a daily making practice. I wondered if they would agree to confront reality with me.

That's where the project started. I observed and listened to my community. I saw a pattern and got curious about it. I believed them and invited them to wonder about it and face reality with me.

I branded our adventure #MakeDontBreak and put together goals and a strategy.

My primary goal was to support at least 5,000 people in developing a daily making practice throughout January 2021. The initial strategy was to create a project with as few rules as possible to keep it accessible, welcoming, and stress-free.

I put the idea out there to see what folks thought. There was a lot of enthusiasm. Then I started getting messages from the community asking for rules. What they were actually asking for was just a bit more guidance. I get that. Structure is important, especially when you feel like your creativity has been diminished by, oh, the stress of a global pandemic and full social collapse. People were tired.

I realized that a daily email to all participants could serve a few functions. First, it could help keep people motivated. I saw that as my number one job. Keep the momentum. A daily email might just be the little spark to keep folks making. I could provide them with something to think about or a prompt that might inspire their making on days when they struggled.

Oh, but there was so much opportunity in these daily emails. I could also use them as a collaboration tool and introduce my community to some of my favorite activists and their work.

I created a Substack dedicated to #MakeDontBreak with the promise that subscribers would get a daily email from me from December 31, 2020, through February 1, 2021, and nothing else and never again. The email list would self-destruct at the end of that period. I wanted folks to trust that this was not some capitalist scheme to gather up their email addresses but rather a gift to them and nothing more.

I emailed 31 of my favorite activists with a clear and simple request: Would they commit to being the featured activist for one day of the month? If yes, I needed the following from them: 1) a photo; 2) a bio; 3) a creative prompt for our makers that aligned with the work they do as an activist in the world; 4) their URLs, social media links, and anything else they wanted to share; and 5) an ask for the community, if they had one. Everyone was on board.

Subject: #MakeDontBreak   MY EMAIL

I am inviting you to a daily, monthlong making experiment beginning on January 1, 2021. You choose your medium. Maybe you choose lots of mediums; the medium is irrelevant. The important part is that you commit to spending time reflecting and making every day for the month of January.

MOST IMPORTANT: Don't make up rules that don't exist. There are no rules. I hate rules.

Maybe you spend five minutes one day and two hours another day. Doesn't matter.

Maybe you stitch, paint, write, draw, collage, metalwork, blow glass, dance . . . whatever moves you to create that day is the perfect medium for you for that day.

Don't overthink this. If you miss a day, shake it off and pick it back up.

Just make! It doesn't have to be "good" or "pretty," and it will definitely not be "perfect," because . . . no such thing. Embrace the exercise. Explore with no expectations. Free yourself of limiting beliefs and just make. Damn it, you deserve this.

BUT WHY, SHANNON? WHY ARE WE DOING #MAKEDONTBREAK?

So many reasons! Some might speak to you and others might not, but these are some of the reasons I think we need this:

1. I have taught thousands of people how to embroider this year, and y'all keep asking me what's next. This. This is what is next.

2. The year 2020 was the fucking worst. I hear lots of people saying, "I can't wait for 2021," as though some magical thing is going to happen and on January 1 the universe is going to right itself. Not going to happen. *But* we can develop a new habit and a new practice while things slowly start to change. This will build up our resilience and keep that hope burning. Plus, with the lineup of folks I have providing you prompts, you are definitely going to come away with some actions you can take to help speed up this change.

3. This is better than a New Year's resolution. And if I hear one person say anything about "losing that pandemic bod for the new year," I will legitimately lose my shit. Developing a reflection and art practice is a much better way to enter 2021 than judging ourselves and making resolutions in the middle of the crisis we are living in.

4. Persistence. How depressed are we going to be on January 9, for example, when things are probably worse than they were on, say, December 31? We need to be prepared for that, and the best way is to work on our persistence. We will do a little bit every day to take care of our mental health, and this is going to help us.

5. Making is fun. Reflecting is invaluable. Put the two together and you have personal growth *and* a super-fun experience.

If none of these speak to you, figure out *your* why, and let's do this.

I started spreading the word through my social media accounts, and soon my community was spreading the word as well. Sign-ups started growing. I sent out a newsletter invitation to my personal mailing list. By December 31, 2020, more than 5,000 people had registered. By January 31, 2021, that number had doubled. Many more people participated who didn't register.

I spent the last two weeks of December organizing and compiling the daily emails for the month. I sent them to each activist to review. Each email started with a personal introduction, and I shared how I knew each guest activist. I wanted readers to feel like they were hanging out with us, and I was introducing them as though we were at a party.

All the content was ready to go by December 30. I left room to write a little welcome message each day so that I could remain responsive to what I was seeing and hearing from participants. After all, the observing and listening had to continue throughout the project to ensure I could adapt and react.

Off we went. And wowwy wow wow did people show up hard! It was so exciting to see the huge diversity and range of creating that went on. I observed how quickly people were connecting with each other on Instagram through the hashtag #MakeDontBreak, and I wanted to provide them with even more opportunities for that, so I built in a Zoom hangout component. Once a week, I hosted a casual Zoom gathering so folks could do their making in community and get to know other makers from around the world. I set them up at different times each week to try to accommodate as many time zones as possible.

In my initial messaging, which I put out in December 2020, I had made a joke about what would happen on January 9 when things were worse. Little did I know it would be January 6 when things got precipitously worse with the assault on the US Capitol building. I sure as shit did not see a full-on insurrection on the bingo board, but can we be impressed by my prediction for a second?

The #MakeDontBreak community displayed a divergence of responses to the events of January 6 (as did we all!). Some folks went hard into making mode to cope. Others were immobilized. I used the daily emails to help those who froze up recover. I reminded them that no one can "fall behind" in #MakeDontBreak. Missing a few days because of the overwhelming despair one might naturally feel upon watching an attempt at a coup d'état is no reason to get down on yourself for tapping out of making. I encouraged them to find just a few minutes to get back to it as an act of resilience, resistance, and self-care. They did.

> **What do you want your legacy to be?** 99

RUBEN ESQUIVEL
@_Esquivel
Co-Producer of The Black Legacy Project.
Artist Manager. Artist.

#MakeDontBreak

#MakeDontBreak Instagram campaign

The month was thrilling. Tens of thousands of Instagram shares used the hashtag, and makers from around the world were connecting. Many people used the project as an opportunity to explore new mediums. Groups of friends got together to make. Some folks ended up carrying on the adventure for a whole year! People are still adding to the hashtag. And one of the most promising outcomes was the connection forged between the makers and the work of the featured activists.

This intervention made a material difference in people's lives. It connected them to a broader community. It introduced them to a diverse group of change agents and their valuable work. It provided opportunities to participate in and support that work. Not to mention that it was joyful and fun at a time when nothing seemed joyful or fun.

I had absolutely no plan to do this until I identified a problem. I observed and listened. I believed what I was seeing and hearing, and I not only confronted reality, but I asked everyone to believe me and confront reality . . . together. Personally, I had zero hope of change happening as the calendar flipped from 2020 to 2021, so this wasn't really my problem. It was, however, a problem I identified and knew that I had the power, connections, time, and energy to offer up some help. So I did.

Keeping Perspective

With #MakeDontBreak, I was looking to put a Band-Aid on a problem I had identified. If I had wanted to go deeper and address the roots of the problem, the challenge would have seemed insurmountable. We were facing the results of a global pandemic that killed millions and upended everything. The rage, despair, and unrest that came with yet another Black person being murdered by police. The tragedy of political divisiveness taking place around the world. And on and on. It's no wonder so many of us were desperate for a sign of progress and harbinger of hope.

As activists, however, it is vital to our work that while we treat symptoms, we also look for the strings to pull that link the symptoms to larger issues. The goal really is to be able to see the wrong so that we can illuminate it for others. We are seers. We are visionaries. Our job is to bring hope, faith, and action to the vision of what can be versus what we collectively normalize and accept. We don't have to solve it all, but we should be working together to create something new.

#MakeDontBreak was a way of shining a light on the impact of the events of the previous year on the individual. It became a way for individuals to reclaim power and take action not just through a daily making practice but through the activism they learned about over the month. It provided an entry point for learning and doing more, for seeing truth and making connections.

Digging to the Roots

Sakichi Toyoda, the founder of Toyota Industries, conceived a simple but effective activity to help us understand what lies beneath the symptoms we are seeing. It's beautiful in its minimalism. You name the problem and then simply ask *Why?* five times. (I'm seeing every reader who has young children in their life rolling their eyes right now because you live this exercise daily.) This process is designed to get you from symptoms to root.

Let's play.

Weymouth, Massachusetts, has several miles of public beaches. I grew up on one and have endless fond memories of crab fishing on the rock jetties. (No crabs are harmed in my version of crab fishing.) We watched the Boston fireworks from the seawall every Fourth of July. The beaches are well loved and well cared for. It is understandable that residents are unsettled and upset by the growing number of used hypodermic needles being found on the beaches.

This issue has played out on social media for years. It's largely people complaining and demanding more of city services while also shaming people who use drugs in some of the unkindest ways you can imagine. It's a toxic stew. But why are there needles on the beaches?

Let's use the *Why?* method and see what we uncover.

THE PROBLEM: There are a growing number of used needles on the beaches in Weymouth, Massachusetts.

> WHY? People who use drugs get high on the beach and then discard their used needles there.

> WHY? It's a mostly deserted spot at night, and they can get high out of sight.

> WHY? It's illegal to use some drugs, and they could get arrested and put in jail if they are caught.

> WHY? The United States has a mostly punitive system in place to punish people who use drugs.

> WHY? There is a pervasive misunderstanding of how and why people use drugs, and instead of working to understand and support their recovery, we criminalize their actions.

Pretty effective little process, isn't it? We have identified that one of the root causes of needles on the beach is simply a by-product of people who use drugs trying to avoid the unsupportive and violent repercussions

My super-
talented
brother,
Brian Downey,
drew this up
for us!

that are a result of our country's system of punishment. We punish people who struggle with disordered relationships with specific drugs.

We can and should make a plan to treat the symptoms of the problem that are putting other people at risk, which is used needles on the beach. But we must also work on addressing the root causes that lead to people using drugs on the beach at night if we want clean and safe beaches again. Punishment is never going to solve this issue.

If we invited a dozen people to do that activity around this issue, we might get a dozen different results. That's why it's so important to work in collaboration with community, especially those most impacted by a problem. Gathering as many perspectives as possible will expand our view and offer up more opportunity. We will come back to this example later.

Wait Just a Minute

In excavating the roots of a problem, we're searching for clarity about its origins and solutions. Sometimes that search means looking behind the curtain of kindness and generosity. How many times have you heard

Who Needs What?

A needs assessment is a fantastic tool for engaging a community to gain further clarity on the complexity of an issue. The assessment is a survey that seeks to understand who is being impacted, in what ways, and what needs they have as a result of the issue. I did some work with a nonprofit working to support the queer community in their city. For two years they had quite successfully met their goals of raising consciousness about and the visibility of the queer community within the city. At the three-year mark, they found themselves unsure of how to proceed to escalate their impact. I suggested a needs assessment. We put together an online survey that invited members of the queer community to identify their most pressing challenges as community members: housing, health care, education, substance use disorders, parenting, inclusive spaces, et cetera. We launched the needs assessment during pride month and kept the survey live for three months. The nonprofit encouraged community members to complete it at all their events, through their social media, and through posters and flyers at queer-friendly businesses and organizations. The data they were able to gather provided them a clearer picture of the community's needs and informed their strategy moving forward.

A needs assessment can illuminate the myriad ways in which an issue manifests within a community. The more voices being heard, the clearer the picture we have.

a "heartwarming" story of a community member who paid off the lunch debt of elementary school students? Or the high school robotics team that built a wheelchair for a young person who could not afford one? Or the stranger who started a GoFundMe for an unhoused person who happens to have an incredible singing voice? These are very kind and generous actions that individuals took to support other humans. That said, when we look beyond the kind action, what we see is the result of harmful systems. Why on earth do elementary school students have lunch debt?! The education system in the United States does not guarantee free lunches for all students. Can't afford your medical expenses? You're not alone. According to recent surveys, Americans have more than $195 *billion* in medical debt. And the number of unhoused people in the United States is more than 650,000, up 48 percent from 2015— a problem that is not going away.

Heartwarming stories are nice, but they often cover up gross injustices. When we can follow a problem to its causes, our work can move beyond just pulling babies out of the river. We can send a team upstream and start deconstructing the systems that lead to the babies being in the river in the first place.

Curiosity Is Key

Identifying problems is sometimes about seeing an immediate and urgent need. And while we may be doing the important work of addressing those needs, often they are symptoms of larger and more systemic problems. To create transformative change, we must get to the root of these problems to ensure that our work is not reinforcing unjust systems and institutions. When we focus on the how and why, we can be methodical and strategic in our corrective actions. We don't have to solve for everything, but we should always be striving for a better understanding of how symptoms intersect and relate. An activist mindset demands that we confront reality and believe others when they share their truths with us. Radical curiosity and critical thinking are skill sets that can be developed, and we must cultivate them in our daily lives so that we can resist the reality that has been normalized in service to the reality that is possible.

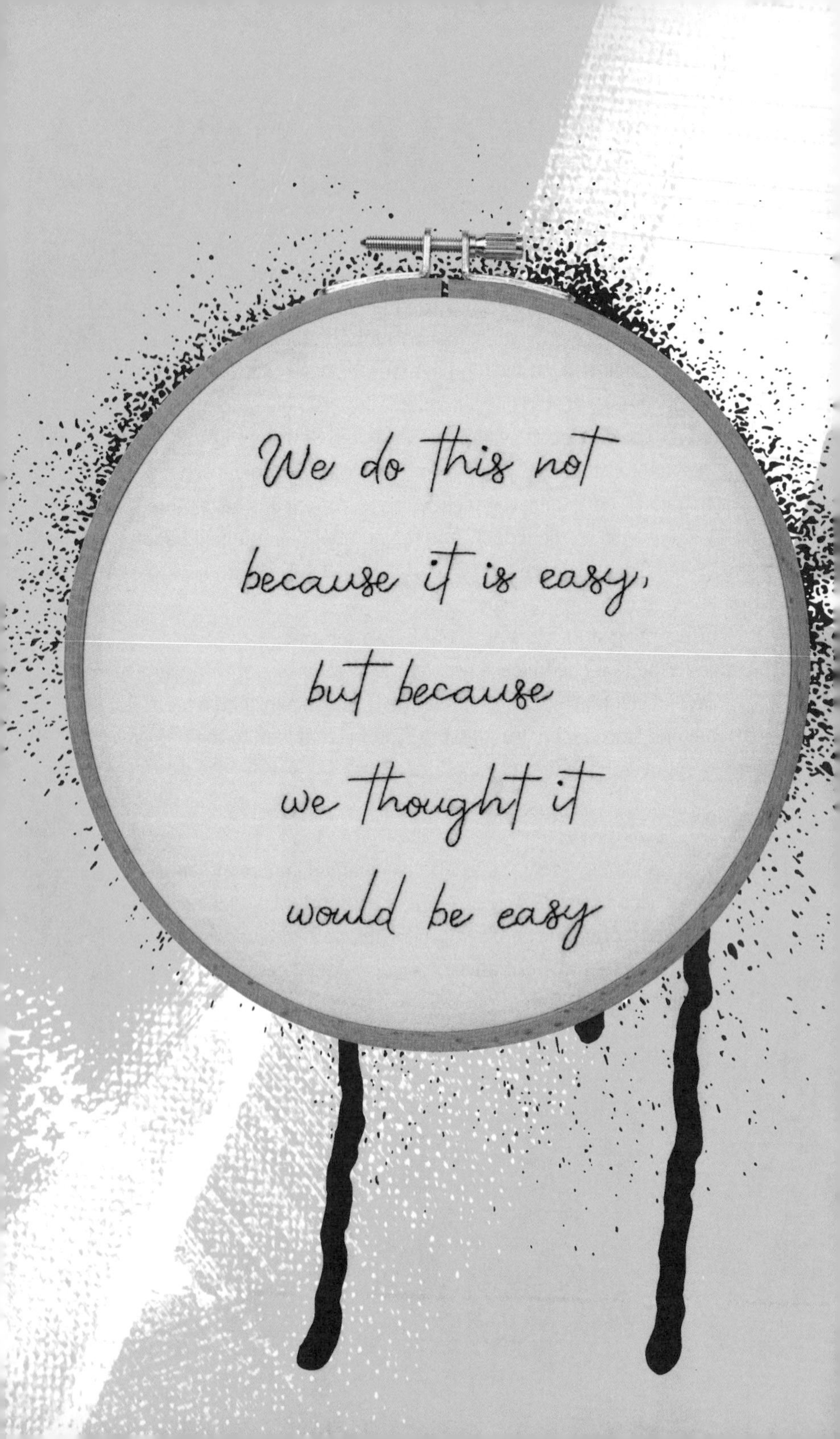

We do this not
because it is easy,
but because
we thought it
would be easy

CHAPTER 5

WHERE ARE MY PEOPLE?

CREATING AN INTENTIONAL TEAM

Activism is rooted in collective work. Hope and action live in the dynamic synergy of groups of humans coming together to work for change. Much of activism is the experience of being in community and working in tandem to bring others into the fold and build unity. This is no easy feat in countries that idealize individualism and autonomy or within organizations that value the status quo. Activism offers us a beautiful opportunity to connect and engage with our fellow humans in meaningful ways.

Creating an intentional team is both incredibly fun and relatively challenging. This is an opportunity to try on and model a version of collaboration that is different (and hopefully more equitable) from most of the human interactions we see and experience in our day-to-day.

This work is not easy. Collaboration is not perfect or comfortable, and it involves conflict, tension, and hard conversations. Reimagining what collaboration looks like is so much of the work. There are no rules to limit you, but there are plenty of models (both good and bad) to look toward as you collectively attempt to establish a dynamic that works. Collaboration in activism is a space to experiment, an exercise in doing it differently. It demands that we shed ego and work to create room for everyone to show up as their best selves.

How do we collectively create a space and working conditions that honor the skills, talents, knowledge, and needs of everyone? Particularly

Accepting help

is its own

kind of strength

Quote by Kiera Cass

when none of us have our baggage completely sorted and we might all need different things? If we knew how to do it, it would be done already! Each group and each situation is unique, so every community that comes together will have to adapt to the current reality. What an adventure!

One thing is for sure: The foundation of success for any group is respect, trust, and communication. Caring about people on a human level is critical to working together to move forward a larger agenda of care. I have worked in several organizations attempting to do critical work to improve the lives of others whose leadership held zero respect or trust for the team—the basic ingredient for a toxic environment in which nothing good could ever be sustained.

To support you in this phase of the adventure, I've put together a nonexhaustive collection of questions and issues to consider as you either build or join a community of change makers.

Why is this group necessary?

Start with the why. By articulating and clarifying the reason a team is being constructed, you lay the foundation that everything else will grow from. You set the intention. Returning to the example of needles on the beach in Weymouth, a *why* statement might look something like *We are bringing together community members to find ways to address the health and safety issue of used needles littering our beach.* It doesn't need to be complex. In fact, keeping it simple and clear gives everyone a starting point but leaves plenty of room for evolution as the group grows and the issue becomes clearer.

Ask yourself whether another group already exists doing this work. There's no need to reinvent the wheel if you can instead find ways to support those already doing the work. Why dilute resources and complicate things when you can consolidate and grow power?

Who should be in the group?

What skill sets and perspectives are needed? Go back to Chapter 3 and the list of roles that exist in the social justice ecosystem (page 88). Does your group have a diverse range of people who fit a variety of those roles?

If you are doing work in support of a marginalized community, are you a part of that community? Is the diversity of voices and lived experiences of that group represented in the team? Who might be missing?

If important people are missing—say, people from the community most impacted by the issue—it's time to explore why that is. Does the existing group structure inspire suspicion, lack of trust, tokenization, lack of understanding of the issue, a savior complex, or something else? How can your group address this issue?

I am often asked how to diversify a group that already exists. It's most often a case of predominately and historically white-dominated groups looking around and wondering why their group is so homogeneous. They want to create a more welcoming and inclusive space.

This is hard. Most people in this situation put in a burst of effort, realize it is much harder than they thought, and then give up. Honestly, I can't think of a single successful example to share here. Why? Creating from scratch with intention is a lot easier than reverse-engineering a problematic culture in order to transform it. This is largely because actual transformation insists that you level it to the ground, dig up the foundation, and rebuild from scratch with a whole new vision that does not center, in this example, whiteness. It requires total commitment from all involved, and it demands relinquishing power.

My friend Mary Morten, president and founder of the Morten Group, has been a leader in organizational development and equity for more than 20 years. I could barely get hold of her after the murder of George Floyd in May 2020 and the consequential unrest and demand for social change that swept through the United States and the world. She was inundated with clients seeking her help to reshape their organizations into more equitable and inclusive spaces, to reshape their work to ensure maximum impact and equity, and to hire diverse leadership. Her team grew exponentially. I had to crash her brief vacation just to get some time with her. (Martha's Vineyard is lovely in July, folks.)

Three years later, in 2023, when I asked her how things were going, she said, "That has all gone by the wayside. The data indicates that people have less interest in anything regarding racial equity than they did before. They are less empathetic and sympathetic to any of those issues. Which is, on one hand, not surprising, and, on the other, I feel like it went so quickly. People came on strong, and it quickly dissipated."

If we choose to think generously about why this might be, we can see it as a circuit overload. Folks who have had the privilege of not experiencing these injustices firsthand got a massive and overwhelming dose of a harsh reality. And, of course, the more you open your eyes to an issue, the more you see, and with awareness comes accountability

SOME OF YOU HAVE NEVER HAD TO FIGHT FOR BASIC HUMAN RIGHTS AND IT SHOWS

Sounds Gay, I'm in!

and responsibility. People who were new to the work of racial justice went hard. It really felt like a tipping point. Then it was all too much. They were confronting more than they had the capability to process and internalize. It was overwhelming, and they quietly disappeared back into their lives where things made sense and they felt comfortable. If we maintain our generous thinking, we can hope that this is not the end of their work but merely a reset.

This rage, action, burnout, retreat cycle can be seen across all issues. Which is why we need to focus our work on a singular issue for our lifetime and be strategic with our time and energy. When we can focus through the lens of one issue we care deeply about, we can see how our work connects to everyone's work. Simultaneously, we build resilience and stamina, liberating ourselves from a vicious cycle of rage and retreat.

That said, the rage-and-retreat cycle does actual harm to those who do not have the privilege of retreat. *How do we diversify our group?* is the wrong question. It implies that there are easy answers—a "Top 10 Ways to Diversify Your Group." There aren't. The question centers the existing group and how they want to demonstrate they are doing better.

Perhaps the questions need to be more along the lines of:

- Who does our group center, and why?
- What have we built that is not inviting to a diverse group of people?
- Are we ready to deconstruct this thing we have built if that is what it takes to create the group we want?
- Why do we want a more diverse group?

Is your group open to all or nah?

Are you crafting a group that is open to everyone, or are you establishing a safe space for a specific or marginalized group to exist and collaborate on issues that directly impact their community?

As a queer person, I deeply understand the value of queer-only spaces. An overwhelming sense of freedom and lightness comes from having a space built exclusively for a specific community. Spaces where you don't have to explain yourself can be incredibly liberating. If you are into documentaries, watch *Crip Camp* for a profound example, in this case of how a summer camp for disabled young people led to the birth of the disability rights movement.

In my own work, I intentionally build spaces to center people of marginalized genders. Cisgendered men are welcome to nearly everything I do, but my spaces are not *for* them. That makes the space a very different experience for anyone who is not a cis man, as well as for the cis men themselves. Honestly, very few men attend my events as a result. That says a lot about the world they are used to living in.

I am reminded of Lisa Woolfork's experience as a Black woman who was part of a quilt guild comprised largely of older white women. Lisa had been sewing with this community in Virginia for years until the "Unite the Right" rally took place in Charlottesville, Virginia, in August 2017. Lisa attended as a counterprotestor standing against the white nationalists and neo-Nazis who were there to protest the removal of Confederate statues. The protest turned violent, and a white nationalist drove his car through the crowd of counterprotestors, killing Heather Heyer and injuring many. After this traumatic experience, Lisa was told that "Charlottesville" was not to be discussed at quilt guild. Her guild returned the check she had submitted for the upcoming guild event, clearly signaling she was no longer welcome. That is violence. After that experience (and I'm sure a million others like it), Lisa founded Black Women Stitch, a group offering an intentional space and team that explicitly "centers Black women, girls, and femmes in sewing while promoting the principles of Black liberation, radical self-love, and social justice."

Sometimes the solution is, indeed, to build your own damn table.

What will the team structure look like?

This is a critical question and sometimes a sticky spot where ego can infect and degrade the power of a group. We are conditioned to work within mostly hierarchical systems of power. It takes a lot of effort and communication to liberate collaborators from that mindset so they feel empowered to be proactive.

A lack of structure, however, can lead to all sorts of unpleasant outcomes, from an imbalanced workload to resentment and ultimately to an effectiveness failure. Structure and accountability are key to outcomes. Articulating how a group can share leadership, the roles folks feel most comfortable taking, and the division of labor are excellent starting points for dialogue and planning. Decentralized organizational structures can keep groups productive without the power imbalances that can come from formal hierarchies. Committees and working groups who have the freedom to make decisions can ensure that group members contribute most effectively. If we all lean into our strengths and make space for others to lean into theirs, our collective labor can be generative for all of us.

When I launched Badass Herstory (see page 71), I wanted other people to not only participate in it but take on leadership roles. After all, the project is just as much a community development experiment as it is a storytelling journey. So the project offers an ambassador component that allows anyone who wants to bring community together around the project to do so, with a comprehensive handbook that explains the project in depth and walks ambassadors through the details and logistics of hosting a gathering for makers. I essentially handed off my vision and invited others to adapt it to their communities' needs.

One of my favorite outcomes was from Cassandra Rosenthal, an ambassador in Portland, Oregon. She brought community together once a week for several weeks to shape and create their pieces. Then the group had a public exhibition of the work before they sent it off to be incorporated into the larger Badass Herstory project.

Another good example is the work of Mindy Tsonas Choi, a trained somatic practitioner who is leading the charge for witchcraftivism. She has been engaging community in Inner Alchemy Collage circles and workshops for years. These collage-centered gatherings serve as creative medicine and are rooted in a somatic approach to craftivism. She is now training facilitators to expand the reach and impact of the work.

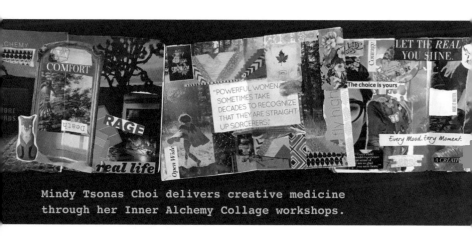

Mindy Tsonas Choi delivers creative medicine through her Inner Alchemy Collage workshops.

How will decisions be made?

Regardless of what methods you and your team decided to use, it is important to have a plan for how decisions will be made within the group. There are dozens of frameworks out there to guide you, but don't limit yourself. Every group and group objective is unique. Some methods to explore include group brainstorming, decision trees, affinity diagrams, importance/difficulty matrix, the Stepladder Technique, the Delphi method, and the RAPID framework, to name a few.

A collective decision-making process is helpful in activism for a few reasons. First, it enables a group to share power and makes sure everyone is heard. The process has a structure to follow but allows a group to tailor that structure to its own needs. Most importantly, the ultimate goal is to find a solution everyone can get behind. The process addresses everyone's ideas, feelings, and conflicts, avoiding nothing, which builds communication, respect, and trust. It demands that anyone who dissents be acknowledged and that their arguments be considered, addressed, and documented if they cannot be resolved. This aids in improving strategies and processes in the future.

The general process for collective decision-making follows a path that looks something like:

1. Issue
2. Share
3. Explore
4. Propose
5. Amend/Solve
6. Implement

Let's walk through a real-world example to help illustrate the process.

Issue

While I was serving as the director of development at a nonprofit in Chicago, one of our male team members was going to welcome a baby into his family. Though the organization had been around for 20 years, this was the first time anyone working there had experienced pregnancy. We had no maternity or parental leave policy at all. Oops. We needed one.

I have never wanted children

Share

Our senior leadership team got together, and we shared our thoughts and ideas on what an equitable parental leave policy might look like. As we were sharing, I started to feel an internal tension. Thanks to our process, I felt safe to explore that tension and share it. I have chosen not to have children. We were creating a generous and robust policy for those who choose to become parents, but what about the rest of us? Do we all not have situations in our life where we might need the support of our workplace to take time to care for loved ones?

Explore

We started to explore that line of thought and worked through the tensions it brought up for us. Issues that came up included the feeling that we were supporting a heteronormative idea of family and our financial director's very real concern about the potential financial implications.

Propose

Ultimately we proposed a family leave policy. This policy was available to any team member across the organization who needed to take paid time off to attend to or care for anyone whom that staff member considered family, be that a new baby, a partner, an elder, a new puppy (obviously, my contribution), and so on.

Amend/Solve

We worked together to establish the language, create a fiscal plan to support the policy, and ensure a shared understanding and support of the solution across the organization.

Implement

Once the board signed off on the new policy, we wrote it into our handbook and training documents and enacted it with the very exciting birth of what can only be described as the most darling tiny human ever made.

What are the expectations of behavior?

When I taught first grade, my students and I would have a brainstorm before our first read-aloud. I would ask them what they needed from each other to enjoy the read-aloud time. Seven-year-olds are so clever and self-aware. Students would say things like "No one should talk while you are reading so we can all hear." One year, a student suggested everyone should sit still so they weren't distracting. Another student made it clear that sitting still was too hard for them, and they needed to move their body to listen. I asked if anyone had any suggestions on how we could accommodate both needs. The students solved it by dividing the sitting space into two sections: The "sit still" section of the carpet

AM I LISTENING,
SOLVING,
OR DISCUSSING?

would be up front and closer to me, while the "wiggly" section would be at the back, and students who needed to feel free to move around a bit could be there. Brilliant, right? We are so very capable of finding ways to accommodate a diversity of needs if we are willing to approach the issues like first graders.

Setting shared expectations for how a group will work together at the onset sets us up for success. We might not always agree, but we can set out with the goal to approach disagreements with empathy and curiosity, to listen to each other, and to always attempt to find a compromise or amicable solution.

Expectations for behavior—you might know them as "ground rules"—might include provisions for the following:

- Stay present and limit distractions.
- Respect each other's time.
- Respond to ideas, not people.
- Allow space for making mistakes.
- Listen to what is being said.

- Communicate to be understood.
- Approach the group with radical honesty.
- Maintain confidentiality.
- Take up space.

Establishing these guidelines is a fantastic first meeting activity. It is both a way to get to know each other and a way to identify the things that matter to different members.

How will you handle conflict?

No matter how much groundwork you lay, conflict is inevitable. That said, if we have successfully organized a space in which people feel respected and heard, then we can expect to be far more skillful in navigating divisions. Curiosity is an excellent approach to exploring tensions. Defensiveness is not. That said, it's a lot easier to be curious about a challenge when it is presented with respect rather than hurled at you like a shoe. Note that this is particularly challenging on digital platforms, where we may not even know the person or may lack context to understand their intentions.

A simple model for exploring conflict in a productive way would be to first acknowledge the conflict. This is especially important when someone is being passive-aggressive, alluding to their unhappiness without clearly articulating it. Once I was working with an organization as a consultant, and one of the team members was *clearly* unhappy I was there. Every single interaction we had was steeped in tension. Leadership saw the issue but did not address it. I am patient, but I am no doormat. When I couldn't take it any longer, I pulled her aside and simply asked her what the source of the conflict was. She looked shocked. She stammered and said she had no issue. I kept asking questions until she revealed that she was concerned I was going to take her job. I reassured her that I was in no way there to do anything but support her work, and only for a short time. After that, she still resented my presence, but

she dialed down her attitude significantly, and we could at least work together. Sometimes that is the best you can hope for.

In that situation, it took me weeks to get to a place where I could address the issue without fear of totally popping off at the woman I was supposed to be helping. Time is a great friend when conflict is involved. A cooling-off period is fantastic for perspective.

Once everyone involved in a conflict is chilled, coming back together to clarify positions is a great next step. Clarification ensures that we truly understand where the tension lives. You know what they say about what it means to assume—it makes an *ass* out of *u* and *me*. Exploring the various perspectives and viewpoints establishes ground to work from as you find a path to move forward.

Sometimes we need to bring in a neutral third party to resolve a conflict. This is why couples counselors exist! Depending on the impact of the disagreement, a peace circle or other restorative justice process might be an option to consider. The important part of conflict resolution is the willingness of all members to bring challenges to the group for them to be addressed. This requires that concerns, when raised, are considered, respected, and taken seriously. We are back to that trust and respect thing.

There is also value to be found in the impasse. If someone simply cannot get behind the solution their group has come to, the process has still provided a wonderful clarity for both the group and the individual. Now all parties recognize they have a core misalignment, and a parting of ways may be in order. It's a gift to be able to get to that clarity, and it should be honored.

What methods of communication will you use?

With 10 million different tools available to us for communicating when we are not in a room together, it makes sense to agree on what works best for the group and the type of communicating you will need to do. Perhaps email works best at the beginning stages of planning, but as the work moves forward and you are executing plans, you move to something more immediate, like Slack, WhatsApp, or a text group. Establishing a consistent means of communication ensures good communication.

We all have different digital communication needs as well as access, understanding, and level of comfort. If you are working with an intergenerational group, these differences will become very apparent, very quickly. Personally, I cannot stand the never-ending "reply all" emails. I will absolutely leave a group if the digital communication feels ineffective and overwhelming. Losing group members over frustrations with digital communication methods is tragic, but it happens, and it can be avoided by getting clear up front and ensuring equity and accessibility.

Go, team!

Cultivating a community of (mostly) aligned change makers is a core element of success in all movements. It should be challenging! That is how you know you are asking the hard questions, digging deep into self-examination and reflection, and moving forward with integrity and intention. The community that drives the work will determine who shows up to support and engage with it. Being part of an effective team necessitates a foundation of respect, honesty, empathy, curiosity, and fervor to establish trust and interdependence. The objective should always be that we are all able to bring our best selves to the work and that we all feel fulfilled and restored through our collective labor, not drained and depleted.

Art-making events offer an opportunity to engage and connect with new people and new ideas!

CHAPTER 6

WORKING WITH WHAT YOU'VE GOT

BRAINSTORMING AND RESOURCE MAPPING

dentifying a problem via its symptoms is the first step. Tracing those symptoms to their root causes is the second. Creating the pathway to change between these two end points is what comes next. Much like if you were planning a road trip from Portland, Oregon, to Portland, Maine, you have your starting point and your end point, but you won't get very far if you don't plan your journey from one point to the other. You need to map it out, build in points of interest along the way, and mark the spots where you will rest and refuel. Where will you stop to see friends?

What weird roadside attractions do you need to experience? Your route might change due to weather, car trouble, unexpected opportunities for adventure, traffic, detours. You get the picture. Things change, and you'll need to stay flexible and adaptive, but you still need a road map.

This next step in our strategic process invites us to dive deep into critical thinking, curiosity, inquiry, and empathy. We explore more deeply so that we can expand our ideas to create substantive change, clarify our resources, and identify power holders whose positions and decisions directly impact an issue. We achieve this through a

PEP TALK

Activism is a never-ending chess game. We come up with ideas, try things, learn from our wins and failures, pivot, adapt, try new things, and repeat forever. Even when we solve some of the problems, new problems will arise. It can be quite maddening at times. The important part is that we all keep learning and doing. Change can be slow and is always incremental. Release any need you might have to be "done" or to "win." Embrace that abolishing systems of oppression is not a one-generation triumph. Set yourself up for success by accepting that systemic change will continue to be the work of generations and generations after you. You are moving the needle as much as you can in your lifetime and leaving things better for the next generation. Trust that they will leave things better for the next, and so on. Hold the vision. Release the expectation that you will see it. #EndPepTalk combination of critical examination, resource mapping, and power mapping. Our goal is to figure out a pathway to change that links the symptoms and the root causes.

Let's circle back to the case of used needles on the beach, which we discussed in Chapter 4. We have identified the problem and analyzed it to its systemic, societal, and institutional roots. How can we solve the symptoms while also ensuring that the root cause is being addressed? That question is our catalyst for visualizing and mapping the pathway to change.

What is the current symptom we want to address? There are used needles littering the beach in our community.

What are the root causes of this symptom? The needles on the beach come from people trying to avoid the punitive and violent repercussions that would result if they were caught using certain drugs. We judge harshly and punish people who struggle with disordered relationships with specific drugs.

We can always
dig deeper.

It's time to channel our inner detectives and start asking questions.

What conditions have led to used needles being a problem on our beach? More specifically, why do people choose to inject drugs on our beach? Well, the beach is largely deserted at night because it is technically "closed" from dusk to dawn. Some of the beaches in Weymouth have substantial seawalls, which create a visibility barrier—they protect people from being seen by cars driving by. Beaches are lovely and peaceful at night. Who doesn't want a lovely, peaceful, deserted, and private spot to exist in? That feels safe. Injecting drugs is an incredibly vulnerable position to be in.

If we look at those informed assumptions and the root causes we articulated, we can take this query further. The summary might look like this:

> Some drugs are categorized as illegal, and if folks are found using them, they will be punished by the state. Therefore, people who use these drugs need to find a space to get high where they are less likely to be caught by the police. Being arrested would result in them being taken to jail, where they would likely be forced into an incredibly painful detox experience. And that is just the start of the hellscape of consequences they might endure because of their disordered relationship with drugs.

Another question we might ask is: Why do people who use drugs discard their used needles on the beach? Some answers might include: There is nowhere else for them to dispose of them. They are high and not considering the implications of their actions. Having "drug paraphernalia" on your person can land you in jail for up to two years and stick you with fines of up to $5,000 in Massachusetts. Folks have no incentive to keep their used needles to exchange them for clean needles because

Weymouth does not have a needle exchange program the way many other cities in Massachusetts have.

See how it works? You put on your detective hat and Perry Mason the shit out of things! Just keep asking questions. I know you true crime fans are excited right now.

Brainstorming Solutions

We have been rigorous in our collective thinking to get to this moment. Now is when we start to brainstorm what solutions could look like.

It's time to call up ideas for action and change. The objective is to take the brainstorm as far as we can from symptom to root causes. This is not to say that this work is all ours to do; instead, we'll work to clarify that what we choose to do is helping and not adding harm. You can imagine how someone lacking empathy and working in their own self-interest might suggest calling public officials and pressuring them to increase policing of the beaches at night. Or organizing neighbors to call police when they see anyone on the beach after dusk. These actions might work to reduce the number of people who get high on the beach, but at what cost? And what change has been made beyond moving the "problem" out of this neighborhood to another spot? Transformative change happens through careful examination, critical thinking, and a desire to create a more equitable world—not simply to make the problem disappear from your view.

A first step might be a neighborhood beach cleanup. This would address the problem that first upset us. Perhaps we even organize monthly beach cleanups, because much like the case of the babies in the river, if we don't find the source of the problem, we will need to regularly clean the beach.

What if we install sharps containers on the beach? This provides folks with a visible and safe disposal option for their used needles.

Decriminalize Drugs

Sharps containers could include resources for people who use drugs. Maybe they could even store some naloxone (Narcan) and drug testing strips. (At this point I will remind you that we are brainstorming. We are not required to think through the logistics of how we might execute these plans. That's later. Think big and endlessly right now!)

Can Weymouth offer a needle exchange program? As of 2022, more than 60 cities and towns in Massachusetts allowed syringe service programs to operate. Weymouth is not one of them. That feels like an opportunity.

Continue to zoom out. Our exploration reminded us that punishment is not a solution, so what is? Instead of pressuring elected officials to increase policing, can we work with community organizations on outreach strategies? We know where people are injecting. Let's activate community resources to be present at the beach to connect, share resources, and support our neighbors who come to the beach to use drugs.

What about that guy who tried to organize the neighbors to call the police and report people on the beach? He is inciting fear in the neighborhood, adding to stigma, and putting people who inject drugs in danger. What do we do about that guy? This feels like a fantastic moment for an awareness campaign. Clearly some of our neighbors need some schooling. A community messaging project might be just the thing to inform, challenge narratives about drug use, and visibly signal empathy and support for our neighbors who use drugs.

We identified the beach as a secluded and peaceful spot where folks probably feel relatively safe to inject. What if there were an actual safe space for them to inject? Could Massachusetts offer safe consumption sites like New York does? These are locations where people can safely use drugs that were purchased elsewhere under the supervision of health care professionals who can test supplies, reverse an overdose, and save lives.

What about the punitive side of the equation here? What laws and policies are causing more harm than help? Is there policy and legislation work that can be done to limit these harms and create pathways to health and stability?

What about the drug industry? What injustices and harm have brought us here? According to the US Centers for Disease Control and Prevention, the number of drug overdose deaths increased by nearly 30 percent from 2019 to 2020 and has quintupled since 1999. Almost 75 percent of the 91,799 drug overdose deaths in 2020 involved an opioid. The opioid scourge has its roots in the capitalist actions of the Sackler family.

We could go on. Remember, it's all connected. Health care, housing, education, mental health services, trauma, employment, and a multitude of other factors all play a role in this equation. The more you zoom out, the more threads you will find connected to the hyperlocal issue of used needles on a single beach in a single city in a single state in a single country.

Knowing the path doesn't mean we have to personally solve everything. That would be impossible. But it can guide us in understanding the people we should be bringing into the work, identifying potential collaborators, naming those who hold power and influence, and detailing messages and narratives we want to shift through our work. A regularly scheduled beach cleanup might be as far as you and your neighbors can take this. Those beach cleanups are to be commended. Even more notable, however, is how you went from wanting to clean up the beach because it was bothering you to an informed group of neighbors who understand some of the root causes of the issue leading to the need for your beach cleanup. You are shifting the attitude in your community (and maybe in yourself). That's what it means to address a problem and the cause of that problem. You never know what you are inspiring! Resilient communities demand that folks know and trust each other. A community cleanup with a harm reduction philosophy is another step toward a connected, supportive, and strong community for all members, not just the ones with beachfront property.

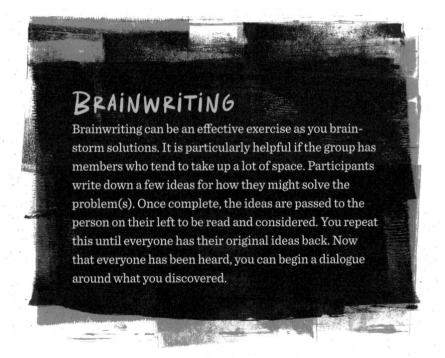

BRAINWRITING

Brainwriting can be an effective exercise as you brainstorm solutions. It is particularly helpful if the group has members who tend to take up a lot of space. Participants write down a few ideas for how they might solve the problem(s). Once complete, the ideas are passed to the person on their left to be read and considered. You repeat this until everyone has their original ideas back. Now that everyone has been heard, you can begin a dialogue around what you discovered.

You can't do it all

Resource Mapping

This point in the process can start to feel overwhelming. We started with one problem, but now that we've dug deep into the roots of that problem, we have a whole list of problems, and big ones at that. We need to get realistic about our capacity to address these issues and identify other resources that can be activated to handle some of the work.

The first step will be the creation of a resource map. A resource map is a visual tool for documenting available resources as well as resource needs that exist. It will provide us with a realistic look at what we can take on. This is how we set boundaries, create action plans, and prevent burnout. By creating a resource map, we acknowledge our personal investment and limits and identify individuals, organizations, and institutions that can add capacity and contribute to the work. We expand our list of possible collaborators.

Whenever I am about to embark on a new project or initiative, my first step is to map out my personal resources. I was recently invited to sit on a board of directors. I do nothing half-assed. I am very committed to fully assing things. So if I were going to say yes to this opportunity, I would want to commit to being a thoroughly engaged board member. I spent an hour mapping out my available resources to evaluate if I had the capacity to join.

First, I wrote out the board criteria.

- Attend one 2-hour board meeting a month.

- Commit to personally donate or raise $5,000 a year for the organization.

- Sell at least 10 seats to the annual fundraising gala.

- Sit on at least one committee, which would entail 5 to 10 hours of work a month.

- Agree to represent the organization at fundraisers and events as needed.

This is a very reasonable amount of volunteer work to ask of a board member for a small to midsize nonprofit.

Next, I examined my current situation against this list. I started with my calendar. I could easily fit in a 2-hour board meeting each month. However, sitting on a committee and finding an additional 5 to 10 hours a month seemed unlikely with my current workload. When I factored in the time it takes to fundraise, coerce people into buying tickets to a gala, and possibly being called on to attend events on behalf of the organization, it was a hard no. I simply did not have the time. I then evaluated my calendar. Were there things taking up time that could be better spent serving on this board? Yes. There were a few things. So maybe it was possible after all.

Next, I went to my bank account. Could I personally donate $5,000 to the organization? Hell, no. Could I raise $5,000 for them? Probably. But that would massively impact my time commitment. Raising money is a lot of labor. Could I sell 10 seats to a gala? Sure. My friends are big

60% OPTIMIST
40% REALIST
100% STRATEGIST

supporters of my work and would buy a ticket or two. But that is another 3 to 5 hours of asking and 5 hours of preparation and attending the gala. The gala would take place in May, which is my busiest work month. So I was back at a hard no.

In the past, my enthusiasm for wanting to say yes would have led me to just say yes. This is a bad idea for all parties. My resource map clarified that I could not say yes. I never just say no, though. I explained my capacity issue, invited them to revisit this with me in the coming years, and offered them the names of other people who I believed would be a good match.

Let's apply this idea of resource mapping to our beach cleanup initiative. Our job is simply to clarify what we know we can personally contribute and identify the resources available to us.

We want to move forward with our neighborhood beach cleanup event. July 5 is a great date for it, since the Fourth of July festivities always leave the beach a mess and it's on a weekend, so most neighbors will have the day off. That gives us two months of planning time. We head to our calendar and find 10 hours a month that we can carve out for planning and preparation. We block off July 4 and 5 to commit to the event. After a casual chat with our three favorite neighbors, they agree to help us. We are willing to invest $50 for supplies. We are members of a neighborhood Facebook group where this issue is often brought up (though not productively).

Boom! A beach cleanup is absolutely doable, even if this is the full extent of resources. We know our resources: 20 hours over the next two months, two days of event work, ourselves plus three neighbors, a relevant Facebook group, and $50. A solid start. We block off time on our calendars and schedule a kickoff meeting with the three neighbors.

Working with what you've got is what gets things moving. Knowing what you need is what keeps things moving.

Know
What You Need

Power Mapping

We all hold power. We can take actions and produce an effect—that's the literal definition of power. You picked up this book and you are reading it. You made a choice, took an action, and produced an effect. You are wielding control over how you spend your time. *Thank you for choosing to use your power in this way. I am deeply grateful.*

We are all powerful. Some people hold considerably more power than others in different situations. Influence and control determine power. When we think of powerful people, we might think of politicians, leaders, or celebrities. They do wield great influence and control. But think about your life. Who holds power in your day-to-day? A teacher, priest, imam, elder, parent, spouse, child, boss, neighbor? Where do you hold power? Influence and control are part of every minute of our lives, from the micro to the macro. Examining power is critical to building an effective activist strategy.

Activism is often about redistributing power in more equitable ways. It is also vital that we leverage power to accomplish our goals. This is why power mapping is such an effective tool in the process of building strategy.

What is power mapping? As defined by the Union of Concerned Scientists, power mapping is a visual exercise that helps you identify the levers and relationships you can take advantage of to gain access to and influence over your target.

This definition, and most definitions of power mapping, honestly, feel gross to me. Thinking about relationships and relational power in these terms feels like manipulations or exploitation for personal gain. Power mapping is perhaps better defined as an exercise in understanding the relational landscape of a particular issue to find collaborators, both likely and unlikely. Doesn't that feel more in the spirit of how we want to move through the world?

Power maps can look a million different ways. The basic idea is that we sleuth out and document who holds power and how they currently yield it around our issue. To use a modern term, who are the influencers?

SPECTRUM OF ALLYSHIP

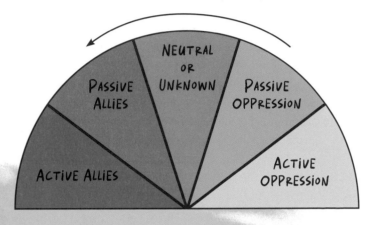

I love the spectrum of allyship model because I like to believe that everyone can be moved along the spectrum if we work strategically enough.

This is our chance to expand our resource base and create opportunity for even bigger change.

Let's look at our working issue, discarded needles on the beach. We could start with power mapping our immediate neighborhood. There is always one neighbor (or a few) who holds influence. Often this person knows all the other people in the neighborhood and demonstrates care for both the people and the infrastructure. Sometimes that care looks like nosiness or dominance. It's irrelevant how it manifests; it's power that can be channeled!

Let's be honest, it's unlikely that anyone is going to be against a simple beach cleanup. You will certainly encounter those who are indifferent or can't be bothered to participate, but outright opposition seems unlikely. This is great! You have a relatively neutral first action, which is a lovely on-ramp for people, especially because you and the team want to move into more challenging territory like addressing stigma or inviting a mobile needle exchange van to the area. Playing it slow and scaling up can move people along the spectrum.

A beach cleanup can be just a group of neighbors doing their thing, but this feels like an opportunity to get city services involved at some level. This brings awareness of the issue to city power holders without asking much of them. For example, we might call waste management and explain what we are doing and find out what it takes to get a special trash pickup for unsafe waste. Perhaps we call the Department of Conservation and Recreation (DCR), let them know what we have planned, and request that a trash receptacle be permanently added to the beach. Maybe we invite our local official to join us. Next, we call the local paper and invite them to cover the cleanup. The outcomes are irrelevant, really. If we can't get a special trash pickup, we can all just take our trash bags home with us and wait for trash day. The point is that we are starting to build positive connections with power holders within the city.

The bigger you go with your solutions, the more expansive your power map will need to be. It is a living document that helps inform strategy. Let's say we cold-call the DCR and are met with a message of

Here's how the beach cleanup team's spectrum might look.

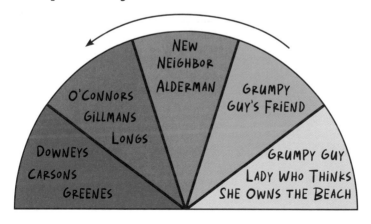

"Absolutely not." Okay, now we know *that* person is not interested in helping, but there is a way around everything.

Another way to power map is to focus on the power holders and diagram their relational connections. Who is connected to these decision-makers? Do they have influence on them?

Neighbor Paula happens to know a midlevel employee at the DCR, and they speak openly about their experiences with drugs and their recovery journey. Can we get to the DCR decision-makers through this manager who is passionate about the issue? Send Paula out for coffee with her friend! Remember, things become more important when people we know, respect, or love tell us they are important. Relationships are the single most important tool for an activist strategy. The power map enables us to see, strengthen, and forge new relationships.

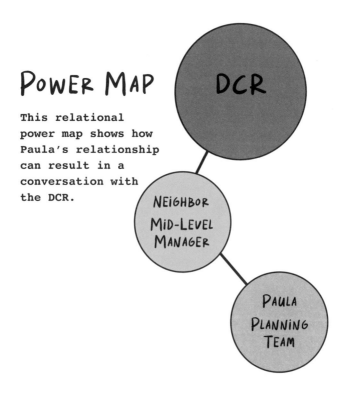

POWER MAP

This relational power map shows how Paula's relationship can result in a conversation with the DCR.

DCR

NEIGHBOR
MID-LEVEL
MANAGER

PAULA
PLANNING
TEAM

Our power map will also help us understand the stances of those currently in opposition to our solutions. We might find that they have some excellent points that will enable us to evolve our initial ideas. Knowing where the opposition stands will be vital later, when we build our messaging plans.

QUESTIONS TO ASK WHEN POWER MAPPING

- Who* is enthusiastically in alignment with us?

- Who is currently in direct opposition to our ideas?

- Who is sitting neutral?

- Who holds influence with those in opposition, neutrality, and alignment?

- What are some ways that we might communicate with these folks?

- Who, in our group, has a comfortable relationship with neutral folks?

*Note that a "who" in these questions might be a person, an organization, a business, an institution, or something else.

You've got this.

As we move from symptoms to causes, we must be realistic about our own capacity. We are in this for the long haul and should pace ourselves accordingly. Through resource mapping, we can make informed and thoughtful decisions that honor our boundaries and ensure we are bringing our best selves to our work. Power mapping lays bare the landscape of resources available to us. We can identify collaborators and networks that, when activated, will broaden the impact of the work without requiring us to burn ourselves out. All of these tools will make your activist life manageable, help you keep momentum, and allow you to remain consistent and steady in your commitment as a change maker.

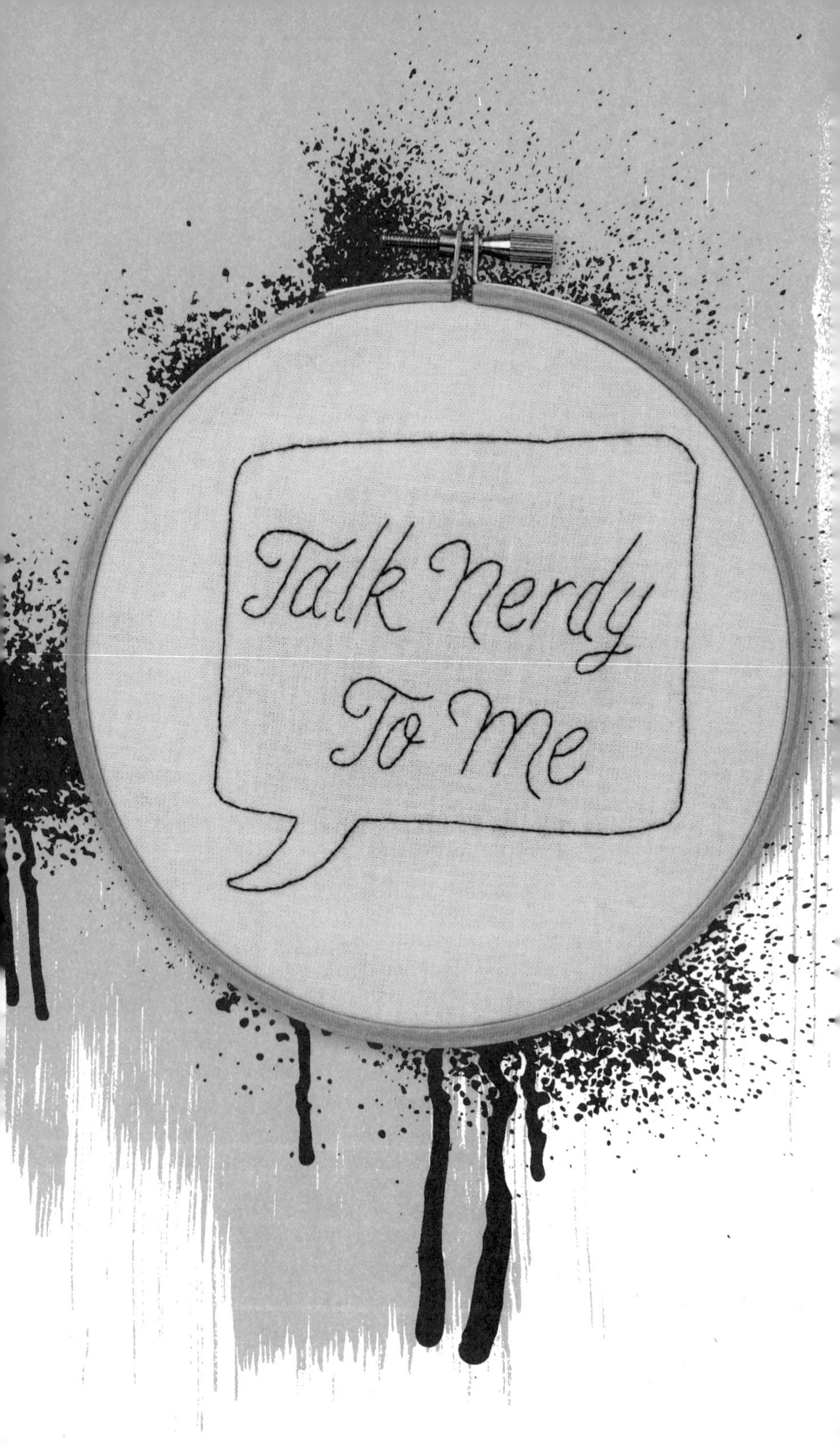
Talk Nerdy
To Me

CHAPTER 7

WAIT, WHAT ARE WE DOING?

SETTING GOALS

o far, we have defined the problem, followed it to the roots, brainstormed ways to solve for it, identified our resources, and established our team—and now we get to set goals! Goal setting is my nerdy nerdy sweet spot. This is when things get real and any overwhelming feelings we might have are washed away in the glory of goal making. The most effective way to make change is to articulate exactly what we want to accomplish. The clearer we are about what we want to do, the easier it is to get it done. In my world, there is only one type of goal. It is known as a S.M.A.R.T. goal.

Get S.M.A.R.T.

S.M.A.R.T. stands for specific, measurable, attainable, relevant, and time-bound. The concept of S.M.A.R.T. goals was introduced in 1981 by George Doran, Arthur Miller, and James Cunningham. This model has been a staple of the business world ever since. Its structure is immensely helpful in ensuring that the goals we set are actionable and helping us map out our action plans.

Specific

S.M.A.R.T. goals are specific. They leave no room for ambiguity. They are not vague. They answer the questions: Who? What? Where? When? Why? How? Creating specific goals leads to either one very long goal or many goals. Either way, the more specific, the better. When we read our goal, we should feel confident in what we are doing and how we will accomplish it. S.M.A.R.T. goals are powerful.

Measurable

These goals include numbers. They are built so that we can track our progress and gauge the success of our outcomes. Having a measurable goal keeps us motivated and focused. We can evaluate our progress against our vision while we work.

Attainable

The goals we set should be achievable. They need to be something we can actually accomplish. Of course, we want them to push us, but they should not ignite fear and doubt. This is why we went through the resource and power mapping activities. We know what resources we have, which we need, and who can help us. We are primed for achievability.

Relevant

Thankfully, we have done loads of work up to this point to ensure that we understand the complexity of the problem(s) we want to address. Making our goals relevant in this context is about order of operation. It means crafting goals that move us along the path of change from symptom to root cause in an order that is relevant to our lives and resources. It should help us move closer to our long-term goals and fit within the context of our available resources.

Time-Bound

Clear deadlines make for clear goals. A sense of momentum and healthy urgency can keep motivation high. Timelines keep us on track and ensure that we are respecting our own time and that of our collaborators.

Here we go!

Let's set some S.M.A.R.T. goals together and get the hang of it. If we were not using the S.M.A.R.T. method, we might state our beach cleanup goal as: We will hold a beach cleanup. That is the objective, after all. It doesn't give us much direction, though. What might a S.M.A.R.T. goal look like for our beach cleanup?

By June 2, we will have commitments from at least 10 neighbors to participate in the beach cleanup, which will happen on July 5 at Fore River Beach.

Is it specific? Yes. We have articulated the support we need, what we will be doing, and where it will be happening. Measurable? Yes. We will know we are successful if we have at least 10 families involved a month beforehand and we hold the beach cleanup on July 5. Attainable? Yes. We set dates and numbers that feel reasonable to us. By choosing the day after the Fourth of July, we have scheduled our event for a weekend and a date when we know there will be a lot of debris to clean up. Relevant? Yes. This event is a direct response to our desire for a safe and clean beach for our community. Time-bound? Yes. We have two firm dates set.

Sometimes, having many small S.M.A.R.T. goals rather than one large one makes everything feel more doable. Plus, few things are more satisfying than checking items off a to-do list! This is one of the little psychological tricks we can use to keep ourselves checking back in with our goals regularly, and it keeps motivation high. A road map of goals offers plenty of moments to celebrate the little wins.

Here is how we might break down the goals for the beach cleanup into smaller pieces:

> By June 2, we will have recruited a 10-person team to plan and organize the beach cleanup.
>
> By June 16, the team will have created a volunteer plan, a supply list, and a schedule for the day of the cleanup.
>
> By June 30, we will have at least 25 volunteers registered and assigned roles for the beach cleanup.
>
> By July 3, we will have purchased or gathered all materials and stored them in Shannon's garage.
>
> On July 5, at least 35 volunteers will assemble at Shannon's house, gather supplies, and participate in the beach cleanup.
>
> On July 6, Shannon will bake cookies and deliver them to everyone who participated in the beach cleanup.

Do you see how setting a series of small goals feels like the start of a plan?

S.S.M.A.R.T. Goals

While maintaining the strength of the acronym, I toss in an extra S, which stands for sentiment-led. How the group feels while working on our goals matters. The experience of the work should come ahead of the building blocks. It is part intention setting, part expectation setting. I know that I am most productive when I enjoy the process and the people I am working with. Therefore, having a shared understanding of how we want the work to feel is a vital component to success.

The sentiment can be a stand-alone goal, or it can be incorporated into each S.M.A.R.T. goal. For example, we can modify our first S.M.A.R.T. goal.

From	To
By June 2, we will have commitments from at least 10 neighbors to participate in the beach cleanup, which will happen on July 5 at Fore River Beach.	By June 2, we will have enthusiastic commitments from at least 10 neighbors to participate in the beach cleanup, which will happen on July 5 at Fore River Beach.

All we did was add one word, but it changes the tenor of the goal. We don't want neighbors begrudgingly agreeing to participate. We don't want them to feel peer pressured, either. We want everyone taking part in the action to be doing so with enthusiasm. Adding *enthusiastic* to the goal may mean that it takes longer to find 10 neighbors, but I guarantee the experience will be far more enjoyable and productive. If we were to add an additional goal centered on sentiment, it might read:

> Participants will feel heard, valued, and appreciated throughout the planning and execution processes. We will conduct weekly check-ins to evaluate our feelings about the experience and directly address any issues that arise.

This clarifies that participant enjoyment is as important to the experience as the tangible outcomes we hope to achieve. It also establishes a check-in habit that centers the feelings and emotions of our volunteer team.

The extra *S* here does not guarantee that conflict or tensions won't arise. But by having a goal to circle back to, we agree that when those moments arise, we will prioritize addressing them and reorient the work as needed. A goal of this sort can reinforce the work you did in Chapter 5 establishing expectations of behaviors for the team.

S.S.M.A.R.T.E.R. Goals

Perhaps you are thinking this whole acronym thing is getting out of hand. To that I say, never! At least when it's in service to making your goals even stronger. S.S.M.A.R.T.E.R. goals take into consideration the very important process of evaluating outcomes and readjusting as needed.

Evaluated

Goals should be fluid. By consistently evaluating our goals, we can assess what is and isn't working in real time. This appraisal process can illuminate places where we need to put more attention and energy. It can show us where unexpected challenges have set us back or require us to pivot. If our goal, for example, is to have 25 volunteers but we learn that many of the neighbors are traveling out of town that weekend, we might have to adjust our expectations to a more attainable number.

Readjusted

As we evaluate our progress, we may sometimes find that our goals need to be adjusted. That could be due to circumstances we didn't plan for, issues that have arisen, or resources we just don't have. What if a storm comes through on July 5? We certainly won't meet our goal of having the beach cleanup that day. Did we fail? Do we just give up? Of course not; we pick a new date, revise our goal, and carry on. There's no shame in readjusting a goal! Try lots of things, adjust, and make changes as needed. Evaluating and readjusting make us more resilient and adaptable to the realities in front of us.

The Magic of the Pivot

In September 2019, I began to make plans to change my life so that I could do my work more effectively. The plan was that in June 2020, I would transition out of my job, give up my apartment, sell my car and belongings, and move into an RV. I planned a one-year, cross-country tour in which I would facilitate community craftivism events and workshops and create art interventions. By late winter I had a map, a schedule, and more than a hundred events booked across 41 states. Then came March 2020. A global pandemic shut down the world. I had

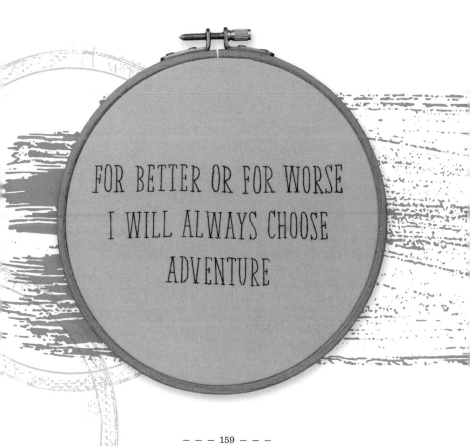

FOR BETTER OR FOR WORSE
I WILL ALWAYS CHOOSE
ADVENTURE

already hired my replacement at work, ended my lease, and started selling off my possessions. There was no turning back. The good news was that everyone was going to isolate for two weeks, COVID would stop spreading, and we would return to life as normal (insert maniacal laugh). I bought an RV and moved into it on June 30, 2020, just as every single event for the first six months of my tour was canceled. Every goal and plan I had beyond quitting my job and moving into an RV was out the window.

WHEN LIFE FUCKS WITH
YOUR GROOVE
INVENT A NEW MOVE

After some tears and copious amounts of red velvet cookies (thank you, Niki), I revisited my goals. At the heart of all of them lay a desire to bring together community to make art and grow as activists. I could still do that! I just had to get creative. I started hosting multiple virtual workshops each week. I was able to teach more than 5,000 people around the world how to embroider that first year. That led to weekly stitch-ups—virtual social gatherings where folks from around the world could come together, make new friends, and work on their own creative projects. Those stitch-ups are still happening at the time of this writing, though now they are monthly. Hundreds of people have attended over the years, and meaningful friendships and collaborations have grown out of these events.

I found ways to bring art interventions to communities. One example was an early partnership with a textile store and sewing studio in Cambridge, Massachusetts, called gather here. During lockdown, we installed Rita's Quilt in their front window so that folks could see the quilt without having to be indoors. I also hosted micro embroidery workshops in parks and on the grounds of various cultural institutions. We were outside, masked, and distanced, yet we were still able to connect and make together.

Next, I launched the How to Be a Good Human series, catalyzed by the prolific increase of xenophobic violence taking place. This ongoing series of trainings and workshops, held in collaboration with experts, offers participants hard skills in service to their development as activists. Workshops ranged from bystander intervention training to identifying and reversing a drug overdose.

As one year turned into two years and wave after wave of new COVID variants ebbed and flowed, I was constantly revisiting and readjusting my goals. It was an epic test of my personal and professional resilience and flexibility. At the end of year two, my RV was hit by an impaired driver, and the accident cost me the RV and many of my belongings. Talk about needing to pivot and readjust goals!

This is all to say, goals are a guide. They are not immutable. They are meant to be adapted and adjusted in service to your vision and current realities.

Potential Barriers

S.S.M.A.R.T.E.R. goals help us identify potential barriers faster than we might otherwise. If we look at our generic goal (to hold a beach cleanup), we can see that we lack a pathway for moving forward and haven't anticipated any obstacles. Our initial S.S.M.A.R.T. goal, however, gives us clues:

> By June 2, we will have enthusiastic commitments from at least 10 neighbors to participate in the beach cleanup, which will happen on July 5 at Fore River Beach.

We know we have one month to recruit 10 enthusiastic neighbors. Well, I know 5 neighbors well and could easily go knock on their doors and pitch this idea. In fact, I feel excited about it. That leaves 5. While I could just knock on more doors belonging to people I don't know, I feel less enthusiastic about that. I also think that some community members might respond more enthusiastically if invited by neighbors they are already friendly with. My strategy then becomes to immediately recruit the 5 neighbors I know and then ask them to recruit the neighbors that they know. Sometimes our S.S.M.A.R.T.E.R. goals help alleviate our personal barriers, too! Like the discomfort of knocking on strangers' doors and asking them for something.

As the group sets the *T* (time-bound) for our goals, we can ensure that dates we are setting work for everyone and don't interfere with things like holidays or school vacations.

Our goals are specific, which ensures we can identify resource needs well in advance and plan for them. For example, if we want to involve city services to schedule a special trash and recycling pickup along the seawall after our cleanup, we will need someone to investigate what is required and make the necessary calls and arrangements. S.S.M.A.R.T.E.R. goals give us the foresight and time to do that.

When we are working at an even larger scale of impact, identifying barriers early and often is critical to strategic success. If you want a little schadenfreude example of the importance of identifying barriers early, watch the documentary *Fyre: The Greatest Party That Never Happened*.

Celebrate the wins.

When I took on a new position as director of development for a non-profit, I was reading through the organizational manual and came across a line that I will never forget: "When we are awarded a new grant, celebrate quietly at your desk." I brought it to my director thinking it was an inside joke or maybe a test to see if I had read the document. Nope. What they were trying to inspire was a sense of celebration for their successes. What it failed to do was actually celebrate. It's no wonder I became the chair of the Fun Committee. Unsurprisingly, I rewrote the manual and leveled up our celebration practices (think cowbell).

The "What's next?" habit is a prevalent pattern in activist spaces. It's the understanding that there is always more work to do. No matter how much we achieve, there is always more that needs fixing. This is absolutely true. It is also soul crushing. Remember the pep talk from Chapter 6? We should always hold the vision but release the idea that we will ever see it. We are here to move the needle and ensure that younger generations are prepared to take over. If we don't celebrate our progress and our wins, activism can become quite depressing. The

I Live for Giggles

process is so much of the beauty and inspiration. Take the time to enjoy the view while you tackle this Everest-size quest.

We must stop and celebrate our achievements. All of them. Honoring the progress keeps morale and motivation high. It also has the added benefit of reminding onlookers that actions make change. Celebration is a very sly recruitment tool. We are in the business of selling hope, potential, and possibility. Constant focus on what is still left to be done evaporates our hope wells faster than almost anything else.

S.S.M.A.R.T.E.R. goals ensure that we have constant reminders of our progress. Each goal met should have some sort of celebration associated with it. I am serious. Life should be fun! Change making should feel exciting and joyful. I have a handmade flag on my desk that simply says "yay!" and I wave it every time I feel like I've done something worth noting. Finished writing a chapter . . . yay! Drank 70 ounces of water today . . . yay! Ran a craftivism workshop . . . yay! I live for giggles. Find whatever works for you and your team, but promise me you will mark your successes and honor your accomplishments. Then take a rest. Then carry on with the next phase of the work.

S.S.M.A.R.T.E.R. Goals = SMARTEST Goals

Goal setting answers the question, *What are we doing?* S.M.A.R.T. goals lay a path and offer us an order of operation for actualizing our plans. By ensuring our goals are specific, measurable, attainable, relevant, and time-bound, we clarify the work and build in milestones to keep momentum. These milestones also provide markers that should be celebrated in our journey. When we add the extra *S* for sentiment, we center the importance of ensuring that the work feels good and the experience for everyone involved is considered and prioritized. S.S.M.A.R.T.E.R. goals keep the work evolving and improving. Evaluating and readjusting our goals as needed keeps us nimble, agile, and responsive to challenges and unexpected barriers. Perhaps the most important role S.S.M.A.R.T.E.R. goals play is informing our tactics. S.S.M.A.R.T.E.R. goals take us from ideas to execution, the next step in the process.

CHAPTER 8

OK, COOL, NOW WHAT?

ur groundwork thus far has positioned us for meaningful and informed action. Without the foundational work, we leave a lot on the table when it comes to change making. This process moves us from constantly leaning on short-term reactions brought on by outrageous injustices to long-term strategic proactive activism with the goal of preventing these injustices. By committing to one issue, you can live your life *and* have consistent and sustained impact.

You are now equipped to develop your messaging and conceive all the ways you will spread that message and incite people to action. You will build a blueprint for delivering consistent, targeted, and coordinated messaging using your available resources. As a creative, you may find this is your favorite part! It's definitely mine.

Words matter.

The language we use shapes the nature of our work. Language is ever evolving, and activists are constantly finding new ways to make our language kinder, more inclusive, and more direct. How we talk about the work and its impact communicates our perspectives to observers.

Crafting the narratives we want to tell is a critical step in carving out our tactics. The linguistic framing of our goals and objectives drives us toward effective tactics for spreading those messages.

In my own craftivism work, I've often created pieces meant to invoke powerful feelings for the viewer. I've made and shared thousands of pieces of art for that purpose. Three of them, each narrative-driven, did some particularly heavy lifting.

I'm So Angry used humor and scale to get my message across during the 2017 Women's March in Chicago. I spent days trying to decide on the message. I realized there was too much to be angry about and I just wanted to stab things (fabric, mostly). I also wanted to feel less angry and hopeless. These feelings and thoughts coalesced into this two-foot sign, which I carried at the march. It led to hundreds of people stopping me at the march to take pictures and talk about the embroidered sign carried in a giant hoop, and it also went viral online. Folks connected with the feeling of anger but appreciated the dark humor that accompanied it.

Boys Will Be Boys set up a sharp counternarrative to the prevalent and prevailing message of the moment. It appeared at a critical tipping point in a shifting culture, connecting with the rage that was being unleashed and channeled by so many through the #MeToo movement. It was meant to be inflammatory, to instigate, and to reflect the outrage that millions of people were feeling.

What Doesn't Kill You . . . was a manifestation of my frustration as variant after variant of COVID surged. I was traveling the country in my RV and saw, firsthand, how differently each area of the country was handling the safety precautions of masking, distancing, and vaccinating. Most areas I traveled through were not taking any precautions. I had given up hope that the situation would improve, and I was feeling resigned to the idea that this was simply our new reality—a reality that valued individual "freedoms" over the collective good. This is the darkest humor I have ever employed. Clearly millions of people around the world shared a similar despondency, as this piece was shared tens of millions of times.

The point is, when we can use our words to connect with millions of people in a significant way, we create opportunities for engaging them in change. My digital communities grew exponentially because of these three messages. My people found me! Through our connection, I have been able to provide them with trainings, resources, and opportunities to further their engagement with change making. My work sent out the bat signal, and hundreds of thousands of people responded. Our words hold power. Craft holds power.

If we examine the messaging of strong modern movements, themes emerge. They are short, clear, powerful, and hashtag friendly. In the digital age, messaging must be able to live comfortably on social media platforms. Social media gifts us a host of ways to build public support for movements. Hashtag activism—the use of hashtags to share and disseminate information about an issue or movement in real time—plays a key role in this ability to unify and connect. It is a base-building tool. It is also critical for interpersonal communication by activists who are engaged in protests, marches, and other actions.

- #AmINext
- #AmplifyIran
- #BlackLivesMatter
- #BlueGirl
- #BringBackOurGirls
- #CounselorsNotCops
- #Cuentalo
- #DefundThePolice
- #GivingTuesday
- #IceBucketChallenge
- #MarchForOurLives
- #MeToo
- #OscarsSoWhite
- #MomsDemandAction
- #MuteRKelly
- #RepealThe8th
- #StopAAPIHate
- #TakeAKnee
- #TimesUp
- #TraffickingHub

These are just a few of the hashtags used over the past few years to quickly connect like-minded people, therein offering opportunities for them to act on these issues and causes. The actions are all different, but the idea is the same: Connect supporters and invite action.

Say what?

Okay, so how do you find your message? The good news is that you have done so much work and thinking to get to this point that crafting the narrative will be exponentially easier than if you just jumped in with a tactical idea. The following process will help you organize your thoughts and develop some impactful messages.

Clarify what you want your messaging to accomplish.

More goals! In this case, you need to establish goals for your communi-cation efforts. These should obviously align with your project goals (see Chapter 7).

Let's revisit our case study. Our project goal is to host a community beach cleanup on the day after Fourth of July festivities. What do we need our messaging to do? First, it must recruit participants. Second, it should set the tone for the event. Think back to the cranky neighbor who also wants to solve for the issue of used needles on the beach. We have a shared vision: a clean beach. We have a different set of solutions to get there, and we most definitely have divergent motivations and feelings about the issue. He wants everyone to call the police. We want a paradigm shift and community care network. The language we choose should make clear our motivations and intentions.

Identify who you are trying to connect with.

Who are you trying to reach? Do you want to connect with more than one audience? The more you can learn about your target audience(s), the better. There is a big difference in how you might try to organize urban youth as compared to rural farmers. Dig in and learn as much as you can, from demographics to psychographics. Don't just focus on their identities and data points; learn about their motivations, hobbies, interests, and passions. Most importantly, learn about how they want to be communicated with. For example, nothing turns me off more than getting random text messages asking me to donate to a political cam-paign. *Never* text me without my explicit permission. I will block you faster than you can blink. My students break out into hives at the idea of someone calling them on the phone. The last thing we want is for our messages to be dismissed simply because we chose the wrong commu-nication method. Become an expert in understanding your audience.

Alongside the methods that you use to communicate with your audi-ence, consider the tone. Will your message be casual, formal, serious, fun, joyful, silly, sassy, or something else? How does your audience expect or want you to speak to them? You can circle back to your power maps to help remind you of your target audiences.

For our beach cleanup, we have a good sense of our audience since we live among them. Our neighborhood planning team will expand this understanding and help us land on an appropriate tone.

Determine what you want your audience to do and how you want them to feel.

Your messaging should be constructed toward provoking actions and feelings. Do you want to educate your audience? Inspire them? Reinforce something? Recruit them? Agitate them? Identifying your intentions will help shape the content. We are going to look at some examples. As you do so, think about which of these approaches inspire you to want to take action and which ones turn you off. Can you identify why?

APPEAL TO THE HEART. I don't know about you, but I can no longer hear a Sarah McLachlan song without thinking of abused animals in deplorable living conditions. The messaging of the American Society for the Prevention of Cruelty to Animals (ASPCA) invokes feelings of sadness, outrage, and pity. They want your heart to break before they step in and invite you to be a hero for these abused animals by donating to support their work.

USE HUMOR. In contrast, the Animal Protective Association of Missouri (APA) relies on a bit of edgy humor to find homes for their senior dogs. Older dogs tend to spend more time in shelters and are harder to adopt out. This campaign is meant to highlight the benefits of welcoming an adult dog into your life as compared to a puppy.

MOTIVATE THROUGH COMPASSION. This campaign from People for the Ethical Treatment of Animals (PETA) uses feelings of empathy and guilt to connect the viewer to the animal being pictured to inspire them to go vegan. The campaign asks the viewer to see the animal's value as a living being and make a significant lifestyle change as a demonstration of compassion.

"NAME AND SHAME." The purpose of this Greenpeace campaign is to directly link big corporations to their role in the plastic pollution issues devastating our oceans. The clever imagery invites viewers to pause and think about their own plastic waste and asks them to sign an open letter to the CEOs of Coca-Cola, PepsiCo, Nestlé, Unilever, Procter & Gamble, Starbucks, and McDonald's demanding change. This campaign leverages the individual's guilt for their plastic consumption and provides them a solution for alleviating this guilt by demanding that corporations stop packaging their products in single-use plastics.

Spend some time analyzing the campaigns and advertising you encounter each day. Investigate what you think they are trying to make you feel. What do they want you to do? Warning: Once you start looking, you won't be able to stop.

What do we want the beach cleanup messaging to do? How do we want our community to feel? We want our neighbors to feel inspired to join in our beach cleanup and immediately understand that our intentions are centered on supporting all members of our community.

Analyze what is already being said.

You will have a rich understanding of how people are talking about the issue from all sides, thanks to your research. It never hurts to do more information gathering. Based on what you are reading, hearing, and seeing, write down the dominant narratives you come across. Generally you can break them down into three categories: *in support*, *in conflict*, and *inquiry*. *In support* describes messages that resonate with how you think and work. *In conflict* are messages that you do not align with. *Inquiry* are messages that you feel unsure about; explore those further until you can more confidently place them in one of the first two categories.

With our beach cleanup, the larger issue that we want to address is drug use in our community, so we can dig into messages about that topic.

Keep it simple but deep.

Words are powerful tools of resistance. Now is the moment to start brainstorming messaging ideas. You know your audience and how they like to be communicated with. You have clarified how you want them to feel and what action you are asking them to take. You've analyzed the language that's being used around this issue. It's time to wordstorm. If you're working alone, grab a piece of paper and just furiously write words and phrases until you run out. If you're working in a group, set up a whiteboard, and people can either write or shout out words and phrases that come to them. If you start to run dry, pull up a thesaurus or word cloud generator and let it fly.

From there, circle the words and phrases that speak to you. Put your goals at the top of a clean sheet of paper or the whiteboard. List the circled words and phrases underneath. Which words or phrases most speak to the goals, emotions, and actions you are hoping to enact? Are they hashtag friendly (if that matters to your purpose)? Just keep going until you've got language that feels like a "Hell, yes!"

DECODING CHARITY

Speaking of the power of words . . . do you use the word *charity*?

If you grew up in a formal religion, chances are you were raised to believe in the goodness of and moral obligation toward charity. In my church, charity was defined as the highest form of love. It seemed legit. However, if we spend some time thinking about it, charity throws down some toxic ideas.

Charity presents the idea that it's our individual responsibility to give to those with less. But taking that concept deeper, is it not also our responsibility to transform society so that there aren't people living without the things any human needs to thrive? Charity promotes guilt and pity while diverting attention and responsibility. Charity often leads to the dynamic of the "giver" being a savior/hero while stripping the "receiver" of their agency and their humanity.

Charity supports the belief that if I have access to resources, I have done this whole human thing right, and if someone does not have access to resources, they must have done something wrong. In reality, we have conceived and built an entire world on ensuring an unjust imbalance of access.

Charity is a whole business structure within capitalism. Religious institutions use charity as a means of proselytizing and as a mechanism to avoid paying taxes—the very thing that could, in theory, end the need for charity by redistributing resources and wealth toward justice.

You remember Sally Struthers and the Christian Children's Fund? Maybe you have seen the Operation Smile commercials? Mercy Ships? Entire messaging campaigns use images and video of Black and brown children around the world, usually in deeply compromising moments, to invoke judgment, pity, and guilt. They point to how little money it would take from you, a person with privilege, to change their entire lives by donating to this charity (often a faith-based institution).

How often do we see white people posting pictures of themselves doing missionary or volunteer work and feeling #blessed and #humbled by the experience?

This messaging is violent and exploitive. System change happens when we can see through these smoke screens, reconsider what we thought we knew, and aim to use our privilege to relinquish our privilege in service to justice.

Are you doing charity work, or are you working toward equity and justice through the redistribution of wealth and resources? It's a paradigm shift worth considering while you develop your messaging. *How* we move people to action matters.

Tactics for Change Making

You have clarified your message. It's time to spread it! Developing strategic tactics for change making is a combination of ingenuity, marketing, advertising, and execution. This is the moment to invest in visualizing how craft and art can help you meet your goals. *Finally! Am I right?!* Turn on that geeky craft brain and let loose.

The first step is to reaffirm the core components that will influence your tactics. Make a list:

> **GOALS**
> **RESOURCES**
> **MESSAGES**
> **AUDIENCES**

Insert your previously established S.S.M.A.R.T.E.R. goals, your available resources, the messaging you developed, and who you are trying to move. This list will serve as a reminder of what you are trying to accomplish, how you want to communicate, and, most importantly, what resources you have available to put toward your tactics. If you don't have the time, energy, connections, or capital, your greatest ideas are dead in the water. Let's apply this structure to our beach cleanup.

> **GOAL:** By June 2, we will have enthusiastic commitments from at least 10 neighbors to participate in the beach cleanup, which will happen on July 5 at Fore River Beach.
>
> **RESOURCES:**
> 10 hours per month in May and June
> Full days on July 4 and 5
> 3 neighbors already on board
> $50
>
> **MESSAGE:** This Community Cares
>
> **AUDIENCES:** Neighbors living within a five-block radius

I like to separate my tactics into analog and digital.

Digital first. We have already identified a robust Facebook group for the neighborhood, and this issue has been raised and discussed there. Creating a Facebook event, sharing it in the group, and asking the group to share it with their digital community would be an easy first step. We could also spend some time sharing the event in other local special interest groups, like environmental or harm reduction groups.

Analog next. This is a hyperlocal action, which gives us a lot of opportunity to have maximum impact without a tremendous amount of effort. We are looking at only a five-block area. We could get together to make posters and flyers and then wheatpaste them throughout the neighborhood to help with our recruitment efforts. Remember, we want 10 volunteers before June 2 to help with planning.

A small community event before the beach cleanup might be just the thing to help neighbors feel connected to one another, thereby making them more likely to show up for the cleanup. We can organize a craft night. Everyone will be invited to come learn how to turn their old plastic bags into plarn (plastic yarn) and macramé that yarn into a bag they can use at the beach cleanup!

As our team grows, we can make a zine that is both an event invitation and a harm reduction educational resource. The zine will invite everyone to the craft night and the beach cleanup. It also will teach readers about the principles of harm reduction and provide information on community resources. We can bring our team together to fold zines and then assign volunteers to each street to distribute one on every doorstep.

We want folks to be excited about the beach cleanup. Let's think how to keep the event positive and energizing. Music! It's time to put that neighbor's garage band to good use. What about some live art making? We can turn the safe waste we collect into a mosaic. All we need is a piece of plywood and some glue. Everyone loves a button—good thing the library has a button maker we can borrow. Let's show some community unity with This Community Cares buttons. Let's be sure to have some chalk on hand so we can decorate the seawall and street with messages and imagery that speak to This Community Cares.

Snacks are always a crowd favorite. Good thing one of our team members is a wicked baker and is willing to make plates of cookies.

How can we, beyond messaging, reinforce the care and concern we have at the event for our community members who use drugs? Let's partner with harm reduction professionals and invite them to come host a table to share resources and educational materials with our neighbors. Maybe we can even get the mobile health clinic to make an appearance and talk about the resources they provide. This would help educate community members and develop important relationships with movement leaders and resource providers, should we choose to expand our work beyond the beach cleanup.

Aren't we clever? I'm sure you have already come up with 10 more brilliant ideas. As you can see, art and craft are invaluable support mechanisms to the goals of our community building event. We have maximized our resources to ensure we are able to reach every neighbor.

Get at it.

As you brainstorm tactics, keeping your goals, resources, messaging, and audience in mind, here are some other things you may want to consider.

What skills are in the room?

A skills inventory is a great way to kick off an initial planning meeting. This is an opportunity for everyone in the room to share both their skill sets and their deal breakers. An inventory will help group members identify the work for which they would be most effective, and undoubtedly this inventory will drive innovative ideas. Deal breakers are a list of things that someone either hates or doesn't feel comfortable doing (or both). For example, someone might be a masterful visual communicator and can brilliantly design our zine, but they would run home if asked to grab the microphone and welcome everyone. We don't want anyone running home. Everyone in that room is a genius, and we want them to shine.

A List of Mediums and Techniques to Get the Juices Flowing

Assemblage / Baking / Block Printing / Buttons /
Ceramics / Chalk / Charcoal / Collage / Coloring /
Comics / Crochet / Dance / Embroidery / Film /
Flyposting / Glass / Graphic Design / Graphic
Novel / Ink and Pen / Knitting / Macramé / Metal /
Mosaics / Paint / Paper / Pastels / Performance /
Photography / Poetry / Postcards / Quilting / Screen
Printing / Sculpture / Sewing / Stickers / Videography /
Woodworking / Zines

How do you ensure that your tactics are accessible?

Accessibility takes endless forms. You will, obviously, try to create events, materials, presentations, and outreach that take into consideration the needs of the individual, not just the many. You won't always be able to account for or predict every need. But by prioritizing accessibility in your planning and inviting your audience to share their needs with you, you demonstrate that creating a safe and inclusive environment is a priority.

I love to use embroidery as the centerpiece of my community work because of how accessible it is when it comes to materials, portability, learning curve, age, and creative aids (patterns and whatnot). Over time, I have learned to incorporate tools and tips to make embroidery even more accessible. I teach learners about using a screwdriver to open and close their hoops if they have arthritis or joint pain.

Planning for Accessibility

Here is a nonexhaustive list of considerations to help you start planning for accessibility.

ONLINE
- Is your website ADA accessible?
- Do you use alt text when posting images online?
- Do you include captions in your video posts?
- Are your hashtags and URLs screen-reader friendly?

COMMUNICATION MATERIALS
- Should you be offering materials in more than one language?
- Is your graphic design (fonts, contrast, color choices, spacing) inclusive?

GATHERINGS + EVENTS
- Have you invited guests to share their access needs with you ahead of the event?
- Are the venue, seating, and bathrooms accessible?
- Are you providing captioning and sign language interpreters?
- Do you have quiet spaces available?
- Are there private spaces for those who need to pump or breastfeed?
- Have you built in plenty of breaks?
- Does the day or time make it inaccessible for people with nontraditional work hours?

FOOD + BEVERAGE

- Do your offerings include *tasty* options for vegans and vegetarians, people with allergies, and people with religious dietary restrictions?
- Do you need to serve alcohol?
- If you do serve alcohol, do you have *fancy* nonalcoholic alternatives? (Water and soda are not sufficient, in my humble opinion.)

MONEY

- Is money a barrier to access?
- If yes, are there options to create greater access equity (pay-what-you-can, sliding scale, sponsorship, grants)?

CONFLICTS

- Have you considered religious holidays that may conflict with gatherings, events, or actions?
- Are there situations that might impede public transportation options? (Just try to get anywhere on the Red Line in Chicago when there is a Cubs game.)

GENDER

- Have you considered the safety of people of marginalized genders in your planning?
- Are there inclusive bathrooms available to the community?

CHILDCARE

- Are children welcome and safe?
- Can you provide on-site childcare options?

I introduce them to needle threaders, self-threading needles, advanced lighting options, and magnification tools for vision limitations. I demonstrate stretches and alternative ways to hold your hoop, including hoop stands, to honor and protect our bodies. I try to always hold events in spaces that are accessible to wheelchairs and mobility aids. All of my self-produced events are either free or pay-what-you-can. And so on.

Are you being environmentally and socially responsible?

Regardless of the issue you are addressing, making environmentally and socially responsible decisions throughout all phases of your process is part of the work. Get into the mindset of thinking through every aspect of your planning with the spirit of closing the gap between your values and actions.

An easy place to begin is by considering what materials you are sourcing and where you are sourcing them from. When sourcing any item, ask:

- Do we actually need it?
- Can we avoid buying it new?
- Is there a way to make it from resources that already exist?
- Okay, we have to buy it, but can we recycle, reuse, or upcycle it afterward?
- Can we buy it from a local independent business?
- Is there a BIPOC-, women-, or queer-owned business we can shop with?
- Have we checked in with our local buy-nothing group to see if they have what we need?

How can we make it as easy as possible for people to take action?

People generally want to be helpful and supportive. The key to getting them to act is to clearly articulate what you need and want them to do. Communication is key. Think through what action your group wants people to take. Then use your messaging and tactics to ask people to take that action. Start small, build trust, and then ramp up your asks.

It is a big leap from "Will you share this post?" to "Donate to our work!" Trust is required. You can speed up the trust building by asking a known and trusted person to ask on your behalf. This is why celebrity endorsements are a thing. Who in your spheres is a known and trusted person or organization that might lend support?

Ask people for what you need, and give them the tools and resources they need to say yes.

WHAT'S YOUR ASK?

- Donate
- Sign the petition
- Attend this event
- Sponsor
- Share this post
- Call your legislator and read this script
- Submit work to this community art project
- Distribute these stickers in your neighborhood
- Use this hashtag
- Submit a testimonial
- Become an ambassador
- Volunteer
- Refer a friend

What are other ways to spread the word quickly?

Think like a marketer: How can you amplify your message and your needs wider and faster? What partnerships can you explore? Would the press be interested in your story? Could you get an invite onto a relevant popular podcast? Should you start your own? Do you need a website? Will your target audience be at any specific events? If so, can you table, advertise, get stage time, or even just attend to network?

When I am launching something new, one of my first actions is to reach out to my friends. I tell them what I'm up to and ask them to participate before the public launch. I never want to start something without some people publicly on board; that's a slog. Before I launched Badass Herstory (see page 71), I asked 10 talented stitchers if they would submit a piece. When I kicked it off, I had 10 brilliant pieces as examples to inspire people. Importantly, I also had 10 influential artists who would talk about the project and their submissions across social media. It is easy for me to ask people to conspire with me because I say yes when they ask me to conspire with them. It is how we do things.

What are the potential barriers and risks?

Risk management is a critical planning component. Thinking through all the possible barriers that could arise will ensure that you have contingency plans. You may need to plan contingencies for everything from material needs to accessibility issues, permitting, counterprotestors, and the potential of violence or participants being arrested.

Security measures should always be considered. Our beach cleanup example involves used hypodermic needles. We need to build in a strong safety plan for who can handle the biohazardous waste, how they will handle it, and where it will be disposed of. We certainly can't have children handling needles. Since we have plans for setting up some tables on the street in front of the seawall, we will likely need to put out cones to alert traffic. We may even need a city permit.

Say it. Do it.

Getting to the doing part is a process of reflection, inquiry, collaboration, critical thinking, and strategy. The process of engagement begins by leading you to explore the problem to its roots, find community to brainstorm and collaborate with, assess the reality of your resources, align with power holders, and set your transformative goals. From there, you can build strategic messaging and tactics that offer the potential for material change. The focus of the work is no longer personal; it is communal. It is no longer short-term; it is a commitment to lifelong change making.

Words hold power and can incite action. Using language wisely is a tremendous responsibility that we all hold, and it should not be taken lightly. Taking the time to slow down and build the blueprint for your messaging is arguably the most important part of this activism process. Having clear goals, understanding your audience, knowing your resources, and crafting effective messaging will make it simpler to conceive effective tactics for spreading your message and inspiring action. The best part is that this process will make every step easier and keep things organized. Your journey doesn't end with the execution of your tactics. We have more to consider and plan!

THERE IS A SWEET SPOT
BETWEEN OVERTHINKING
AND UNDERPLANNING
WHERE YOU JUST START DOING

×

CHAPTER 9

WELL, THAT WAS FUN

MILESTONES, TIMELINES, AND ASSESSMENTS

E very project, event, or action requires a strong organizational system to be successful. Brilliant ideas collapse under the weight and frustration of disorganization. Establishing a strong organizational plan ensures that we are meeting our goals, evaluating our progress, making changes as needed, and maintaining momentum.

People generally have two kinds of reactions to the idea of spreadsheets: First, elation, from my fellow spreadsheet-loving nerds. Second, sinking dread, from my *please don't make me open any spreadsheets* friends. For the latter, I have excellent news: *You* don't have to open any spreadsheets. Nobody needs to try to do it all, and none of us should force ourselves to do things we despise. There are so many potential collaborators who perk right up upon hearing the words *project management*. Let's rely on them for spreadsheet work. If organization is not your strong suit, make sure the team you create or join has plenty of the Marie Kondo types.

Organization is simply a way to respect our time and resources. It is a display of reverence for ourselves, our collaborators, and the work. When we set boundaries—which is really what being organized is about—we communicate our values.

Here we are going to explore ways to develop and manage simple organizational systems to support the work, keep us accountable, and infuse celebration. You have already done the lion's share by establishing your S.S.M.A.R.T.E.R. goals, building your resource map, and naming your tactics. Now it is just a matter of identifying your needs and laying out the action plan.

Establishing Action Steps

As much as I love a spreadsheet and can manage a calendar like nobody's business, my brain rejects all organizational software and templates. Seriously, I've never met an app that fits my needs or feels intuitive to use. I value simplicity, clarity, and ease. So I just make my own tools. Getting organized doesn't have to be complicated.

The first step is to use your S.S.M.A.R.T.E.R. goals to build a timeline. As mentioned in Chapter 7, breaking down your primary goal into many makes it easier to build a timeline. Let's look at the beach cleanup goals.

> By June 2, we will have recruited a 10-person team to plan and organize the beach cleanup.
>
> By June 16, the team will have created a volunteer plan, a supply list, and a schedule for the day of the cleanup.
>
> By June 30, we will have at least 25 volunteers registered and assigned roles for the beach cleanup.
>
> By July 3, we will have purchased or gathered all materials and stored them in Shannon's garage.

On July 5, at least 35 volunteers will assemble at Shannon's house, gather supplies, and participate in the beach cleanup.

On July 6, Shannon will bake cookies and deliver them to everyone who participated in the beach cleanup.

Because we set S.S.M.A.R.T.E.R. goals, we already have benchmarks to build from. Let's put them in a simple two-column spreadsheet.

DATE	ACTION
June 2	10 volunteers on board
June 16	Volunteer plan, supply list, day-of schedule
June 30	25 volunteers registered w/roles for 7/5
July 3	All supplies secured and in Shannon's garage
July 5	35+ volunteers participate in cleanup

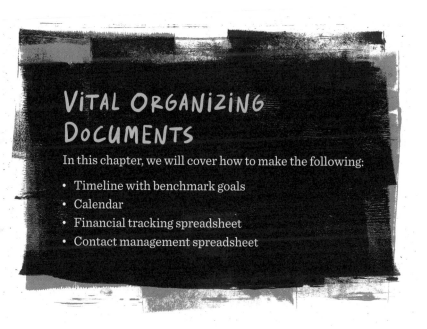

VITAL ORGANIZING DOCUMENTS

In this chapter, we will cover how to make the following:

- Timeline with benchmark goals
- Calendar
- Financial tracking spreadsheet
- Contact management spreadsheet

Now we can work backward to identify the action steps we need to take to ensure we meet these deadlines. I usually start by brain-dumping the actions and then go back and organize them.

Looking at our first goal, we have one month to get 10 volunteers on board. We already have 3 volunteers, thanks to our neighborhood friends. Together, we decided flyers would be an effective tactic to both recruit planning volunteers and encourage the community to show up on July 5. What actions need to take place?

- Make the flyer.

- Photocopy the flyer.

- Post flyers throughout the neighborhood.

As a group, drill down into each action and start assigning responsibilities.

MAKE THE FLYER

WHO: Who has the time and skills to make the flyer?
WHAT: What information needs to be included on the flyer?
WHEN: When do we need the flyer to be ready to go?

PHOTOCOPY THE FLYER

WHO: Who has the time and resources to copy the flyers?
WHEN: When do we need all these copies ready to go?

POST FLYERS THROUGHOUT THE NEIGHBORHOOD

WHO: Who has the time and resources to post the flyers?
HOW: Who has the time and resources to make the wheatpaste and gather the materials?
WHEN: On what day should we post the flyers?

We'll add all these action steps and details to our spreadsheet.

As we discuss what information needs to be on the flyer, we realize that we need a point of contact for volunteers. This person will need to have time to correspond with volunteers and a spreadsheet to keep track of names and contact information. We'll add this information to our spreadsheet, too.

DATE	ACTION	TEAM MEMBER
May 2	Recruitment meeting at Shannon's house	Jenn, DuShaun, Melissa
May 9	Flyer completed	Melissa
May 10	Staples to photocopy 100 flyers	Jenille
May 15	Wheatpaste made, materials gathered, streets assigned	Shannon
May 16	Flyer posting day	Jenn, Jenille, Melissa, Shannon
May 16—June 2	Volunteer correspondence	Jenn
June 2	10 volunteers on board	

Boom! We have our action steps to meet our first goal. Now, we'll add the resources we will need along the way.

Respecting your time is Respecting yourself

DATE	ACTION	TEAM MEMBER	TIME	COST
May 2	Recruitment meeting at Shannon's house	Jenn, DuShaun, Melissa	1 hour	
May 9	Flyer completed	Melissa	1 hour	
May 10	Staples to photocopy 100 flyers	Jenille	.5 hour	$20.00
May 15	Wheatpaste made, materials gathered, streets assigned	Shannon	1.5 hours	$8.00
May 16	Flyer posting day	Jenn, Jenille, Melissa, Shannon	2 hours	
May 16– June 2	Volunteer correspondence	Jenn	1.5 hours	
June 2	10 volunteers on board			

You can use the same process to map out action steps for any activism project. Break down your goals, create a timeline, and map out the action steps. Soon you will have a robust plan. This living document will guide all your actions. Each time you meet a goal or come up to a deadline, evaluate how things went and adjust as needed.

For example, if it is one week out from our June 2 deadline and we have only eight volunteers signed on, it is time to come up with a new recruitment tactic. The flyers were successful in recruiting five additional volunteers, but the deadline is fast approaching. It's time for our eight volunteers to reach out to at least two neighbors they know and ask them to join in the fun.

Benchmark goals ensure we are on track to meet our overall objective: a well-attended beach cleanup. Our timeline builds in accountability as team members move forward to take on specific responsibilities. It also sets the important due dates so that we can build out a project calendar.

The timeline also serves as a reminder of moments to celebrate! When you meet a goal, find a way to celebrate that win. I build micro celebrations right into timelines, so we all have something tangible to look forward to. I am very food motivated, so my celebrations mostly involve pizza and baked goods. I've been known to celebrate by holding an impromptu dance party, distributing craft supplies, making ridiculous awards and trophies, banging a cowbell, and giving gift certificates to local businesses.

DOCUMENT IT ALL

Document, document, document. Consistent assessment of your process and progress will enable real-time adjustment. It will also make it easier to prove success and learn from failures. Beyond the more formal documents we discuss in this chapter, I suggest keeping an archive of agendas, meeting notes, brainstorms, marketing collateral, photographs, videos, testimonials, and anecdotals. These resources will be invaluable moving forward. They will make it easier to tell your story and share your successes with others. It is important to share what you have done and learned with others! It's not bragging. It's power building. It's base building. It's inspiring. Document and share your story. Let us learn with and from you. This is how you move people.

Get it all on the calendar.

Next, take that beautiful timeline and get it on a calendar. Calendars help us manage our time, set boundaries, ensure that we have ample time to rest and play, and meet deadlines.

You already identified what communication methods your team prefers. Now add calendars to that exploration. Find the solution that works for everyone. For collaborative and team projects, shared online calendars are especially effective. They allow a team to manage their own work and keep tabs on overall progress. If the team has a shared working space, a big analog wall calendar is a great visual reminder of your progress and upcoming tasks.

Calendars can be very helpful with stress management. Knowing when we need to put our attention to something ensures that we don't unnecessarily spend time thinking about it before we must. (You will often hear me say things like "That's not a today problem" or "That's a July problem.") We can simply focus on the now and trust that we'll deal with the future activities when it's time.

However you do it, a well-managed calendar is an imperative.

Managing Money

A financial tracking spreadsheet is another imperative, regardless of how much funding you are working with. From $50 to $5 million, you should be keeping tabs on every dollar. The most basic rationale for keeping a budget is to ensure you have the resources to accomplish the work. Clear financials help in more strategic ways, too. Whether you like it or not, funding can largely dictate your strategic path. Your future tactical plans might require far more funding than you currently have. Projecting costs for each step of the plan shows you when and how much fundraising to do. Importantly, if you will need to do fundraising in the future, being able to demonstrate past success both through impact and fiscal responsibility is an important part of the story. Everyone wants to ensure their money will be put toward impactful change. Grant funding is particularly numbers driven.

A budget is also helpful in determining where you must spend money and where you can find workarounds. For example, at the start of the beach cleanup project, we had $50 in funds. By the end of the

first month, we were down to $22. That doesn't leave much for supplies. Knowing this in advance, we have options. We can do a little fundraising by asking each volunteer if they would kick in some cash. We could have a donation jar at the actual event and hope that we recoup any extra costs. We can look at the supply list and find ways to get the things we need without spending money. I imagine that in a five-block area in the suburbs of Boston, you can find just about anything you might need simply by asking neighbors.

Again, you don't have to be the one building and managing the budget. But everyone on the team should understand the financials and be updated on the budget regularly (and often).

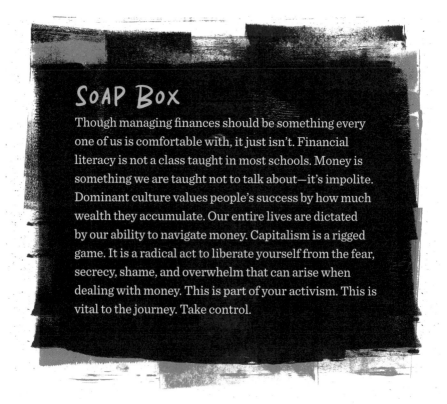

SOAP BOX

Though managing finances should be something every one of us is comfortable with, it just isn't. Financial literacy is not a class taught in most schools. Money is something we are taught not to talk about—it's impolite. Dominant culture values people's success by how much wealth they accumulate. Our entire lives are dictated by our ability to navigate money. Capitalism is a rigged game. It is a radical act to liberate yourself from the fear, secrecy, shame, and overwhelm that can arise when dealing with money. This is part of your activism. This is vital to the journey. Take control.

Contacts

The last vital organizing document is your contact list. Connections are key. You will need a comprehensive contact management system. There are plenty of apps and tools out there to manage contacts. A search for "CRM software" will get you far. You can always build your own system in whatever software you prefer. The basic details to include for any contact are name (spelled correctly), email, phone number, address, and social media handles.

I am absolute garbage at remembering people's names. I can tell you a hundred random facts about everyone I've ever met with zero effort, but recalling names is my weakest skill set. Therefore, all my contacts include notes and bits of information about each person. For example, John: lighting designer, Las Vegas, made those amazing LED costumes for Cirque, loves cats, husband is Mac, votes, donates, funny af, memes welcome. I add notes every time I interact with people. My spreadsheets usually have two extra columns: "Past Actions" and "Future Requests." In the past actions column, I document what people have done for the project, organization, or action—whether they attended an event, donated, amplified, volunteered, or whatever. I try to be as specific as possible. In the future requests column, I list the next actions I would like them to take so that I can remember to ask them.

Every person, business, and organization you reach out to should be included in your spreadsheet. The notes are particularly important. For example, it is common for small businesses to want to support an event, but the timing is off. They might encourage you to circle

ASK FOR WHAT YOU NEED

back to them in the fall for a donation. You are responsible for remembering to do that.

Again, this is a situation where a shared spreadsheet or system is imperative. The team should all have access to the contact list and be responsible for inputting and updating information as you go.

Our beach cleanup contact list would start with our organizing team. As people register for the event, we will gather their contact information. On the day of the beach cleanup, we will have a registration table, and everyone who shows up to help will be invited to share their contact information for future events.

What's next?

The farther out you can vision, the more strategic you can be at every stage of the process.

When you can envision what is possible, the mission to achieve that vision shapes and reshapes your work, words, ideas, and collaborations. The more you try, the more you learn. As you implement your messaging and tactics, you will learn what works and what doesn't. That is why the E.R. of your S.S.M.A.R.T.E.R. goals matters so much. Evaluating your process and progress provides the opportunity to readjust.

After a campaign or action, gather (in person, if possible) to celebrate and evaluate. Like stretching after a workout, the debrief is often skipped yet is critical to future progress. Kick it off with joy, honoring all the contributions. Find creative ways to uplift accomplishments.

Next, pull from your formal documentation. Did you meet your goals? What were barriers that arose? Look at the hard numbers. How did your funding fare? How many volunteers, participants, and/or attendees did you have? Look at all your metrics.

Don't just look at spreadsheets, though. How did everyone feel throughout the process? As the 1980s glam metal band Poison proclaimed, every rose has its thorn. What were the highs and lows of the experience? Share anecdotals. What did people say about their participation? What sort of emails, texts, tweets, or other messages did you receive?

Summarize the takeaways from the debrief. When you are ready to start planning your next moves, review the debrief. Use it to inform your next steps.

Escalate, pivot, iterate, or quit.

Congratulations! You did it. The process is complete. Now it's time to consider how you want to move forward. Radical honesty is required.

Escalate

You did the thing. You have celebrated and rested. You are ready for more. What is your next inspired action? I generally find that an intuitive next step presents itself. When you are in the work, the work has a way of showing you the path forward. That is largely thanks to community. When people see what you are up to, new collaborations and opportunities arise.

If you feel unsure what your next move should be, revisit your brainstorms (which, of course, you documented and stored for just this moment). You likely already have a next step just waiting for you. Thank your past self for that one!

Still unsure? Circle back to the brainstorming part of the process and do it again. That's the glory of having a strategic process to follow: You always have somewhere to turn. Once you have your idea, it's back to goal setting, resource mapping, developing your messaging and tactics, and doing the damn thing.

Returning to our beach cleanup example, the event was successful. We met our goals, had a joyful time, and ate success cookies, and the volunteer team is ready for more. One of our biggest takeaways from the experience was seeing firsthand how pervasive the stigma around drug use is. Even well-meaning neighbors were using harmful language and leaning on stereotypes. We decide that an educational campaign is in order. We are only a month and half away from International Overdose Awareness Day, which feels like a perfect moment to launch a campaign. Time to set some goals and make some plans!

Pivot

Did you learn something critical, encounter a barrier, or come upon a new opportunity through your experience? Perhaps a pivot is in order. While having a long-term plan is important, it's good not to cling to it tightly. Being flexible, responsive, and willing to adapt has a profound impact on your future success.

Let's say that after the beach cleanup, we planned on focusing our efforts on building and installing a sharps receptacle on the beach. This artistic structure would be complete with naloxone (Narcan), testing strips, and an educational zine with a list of needle exchange sites and

LET IT SPARK JOY

Organizational tools power our strategic work. They ensure that we are on track and respecting everyone's time, and they make it far easier to know when to say yes and when to say no. Being organized sets us up for success as we evaluate and readjust our work to meet our goals and serve our mission. Through documentation, we can tell robust stories of process and success. As we assess and reflect, our documents support our inquiry and the prioritization of what our next steps should be. Find the people who love this part and let them shine!

other important local resources. But the powers that be tell us we absolutely cannot do that on a public beach. There are no city resources for safely emptying and disposing of sharps. Frustrating but predictable. The good news is, we are in communication with the power holders. We can shift our energies toward working with (or pressuring) the city to incorporate these services into their budget. By working toward citywide or statewide changes, we can have an even bigger impact. It is likely that this path will keep us pivoting as we start to address institutional change. New ideas will develop as we encounter barriers and find the cracks. Embrace the pivot and carry on. We may not get our beach structure for sharps disposal, but we can certainly use the process to push for other important changes.

Iterate

Is the plan to repeat the event, project, or action? Fabulous. What needs to change to make the next one an even bigger success? Your documentation and organizational systems are going to be critical. Do you need to fundraise? Add more team members? Change the location? Move the date? Learn from your previous experiences, rely on your documentation, and continue to evolve the work. You have the process and the groundwork. It's just onward and upward from here.

Quit

Can you even believe I said that? Real talk: Sometimes things just don't work. Fails are part of the learning process. The tricky part is seeing it for what it is and letting it go. There are a million reasons an idea might not work. Learn from it, but don't dwell on it. There is work to be done, and you will find a new way.

Conversely, you could have had an epic success that simply cannot or should not be repeated. It was a moment. Take the win and let it go.

The Power of Youth: A Case Study

Asian Americans Advancing Justice | Chicago is a nonprofit working toward racial equity through collective advocacy and organizing. They run a very successful youth program called KINETIC, which came about when the organization was assessing their work within the Asian American community and realized that the voice of young people was not represented in a meaningful way.

In response, a civic engagement curriculum was developed in 2010 and delivered in English Language (EL) classrooms in several public schools throughout Chicago. Students were not just learning the English language; they were learning how to wield the power of language to advocate for their rights and to create change in their schools and communities—and thus challenging the idea of who gets to hold power. The curriculum leaned heavily on art, culture, and media. It included culturally relevant texts, self-authorship and expression, and media literacy as a way to help students reimagine schools in their city.

KINETIC's work grew exponentially over the years as a direct result of listening to students and supporting them in their growth as community leaders. Through inquiry, students identified several issues they faced as immigrants, refugees, undocumented people, and English-language learners within the Chicago public schools.

KINETIC youth specifically identified the following pressing issues as barriers to their vision of fully resourced schools that support all learners:

- Students were regularly being pulled out of their classes to interpret for community members and parents when no one on staff could speak the presenting language.

- Students were being asked to interpret for their peers who were less proficient in English within the classroom.

At the annual KINETIC art show, students in Chicago share art that portrays the joys and complexities of being an immigrant or refugee student.

- Most EL students were not able to take any electives. On top of their EL classes, they were required to take an additional world language class. In other words, students who were already fluent in one non-English language (or many languages) were now learning English and also required to study another language. This meant they had no time in their schedules for other electives like art or music.

The KINETIC leadership (staff and youth) decided to host what became an annual art show. Art, they agreed, was a mechanism for communicating that did not require them to lean on any particular spoken language. They were able to expertly share their lived experiences and struggles within the educational system—no translation needed.

Hundreds of students from across Chicago submitted art that illustrated and highlighted the beauty, complexity, joy, and struggles of being an immigrant or refugee student and person. The work demonstrated the similarities and differences in experiences across cultures and languages. It was a powerful consciousness-raising experience that offered up endless counternarratives to common (mis)conceptions about immigrants and refugees.

The annual art shows are centered on specific themes, such as:

- *Suitcase: The Power We Carry*, which alluded to the students' lived experiences as immigrants—many had immigrated to the United States with just a suitcase—while also demonstrating that those lived experiences granted them strength and power

- *Ctrl Alt Delete*, which spoke directly to students' desire to erase problematic narratives about their communities—that is, the narratives being encouraged by the white supremacist and xenophobic government leadership

The youth leadership worked alongside the KINETIC programming staff to develop a list of demands that would create a more equitable, just, and safe educational experience for them. Students then created

Students lead the creative calls to action based on their needs and demands.

a power map and identified the vast range of power holders in their schools, school district, neighborhood, city, and state. They sent invitations and personal asks to all of them. They employed social media to spread the messaging and drive attendance.

KINETIC youth were tasked with establishing organizational systems, and the development team (myself included) worked with them on fundraising for the event through sponsorship opportunities, grants, and individual donations. They managed the budget and learned how to allocate resources along priority lines.

Every year, the venue has had to change to accommodate the growth of the event. Teachers, principals, religious leaders, elected officials, community leaders and members, families, and students pack the venue for this one-night-only event. Beyond the art, KINETIC youth leaders take the stage to share their experiences and their demands to bring attention to what needs changing in their classrooms and schools.

The team documents their process and the event extensively. Lots of selfies, photographs, and videos are taken. The art show is the highlight of the year, galvanizing students and serving as a recruiting method for the intensive summer program. Fundraising has gotten easier over the years as the history of and stories from the events have demonstrated growth and impact.

In 2018, KINETIC leaders won their campaign to change the world language requirement for English learner students, and their annual art show played a major role in that success. The very same students who were denied access to the arts in school were able to use art and craft to communicate and advocate for their needs.

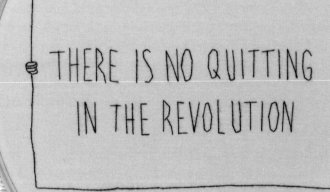

CHAPTER 10

TO SUM IT UP

THE ACTIVIST LIFESTYLE

The work of social change can be freaking exhausting. It is endless, and it's easy to lose sight of the impact you are having when change seems so slow. Burnout and empathy fatigue are real.

I have been in the dark places. I have wanted to give up. It took 20 years for me to find the solutions to keep me centered and moving forward. Now, I live in a space of near constant motivation. I got here by relinquishing the need to control things. I confronted reality and accepted it. As a young activist, I really believed I would see a just world in my lifetime. That amorphous grand vision made it impossible for me to see the progress being made. It made it impossible to see the finish line. Now, I realize I'll never see the finish line or the winner's podium (here we go again with the running analogies). I'm a leg in a relay race. My job is to move us forward with as much speed as I can muster and hand the baton off to the next generation. This understanding liberated me.

It also reshaped how I thought about spending my years on this planet. The heart of what I do is move people from being passive consumers to engaged creators. I leverage craft-based art forms to welcome community in, support them in learning new things, and invite them to use their new skills to identify and articulate what matters to them. As we build a bond of trust and wonder, I encourage them to use their voices and skills to take action on the issues they care about most, transitioning them from makers to change makers. My work is about telling the truth while simultaneously inspiring radical hope. It's about confronting harsh realities and finding the pathways to change. It's about motivating every single person I meet to want to have a positive impact and walk away feeling empowered and downright excited about what is possible. I hope to inspire a sense of curiosity, inquiry, and critical thinking through both my own artistic practice and my community practices. In a nutshell, I recruit and support burgeoning activists.

Through this understanding, I know what success looks and feels like for me. I know my mission, which makes it exponentially easier to set goals. The path is clear, and anything that steers me off course earns a firm and confident "No, thanks." When forced detours occur (hello, global pandemic), I can adapt because where I'm headed hasn't changed. The greatest outcome is the peace and comfort I carry knowing that I am doing everything I can. I can see and honor the progress being made.

Throughout our journey together, you have done extensive self-reflection and critical thinking. It's time to translate all those ideas into your very own vision and mission statements. These statements will guide your efforts and support you in setting boundaries. We want to create an activist lifestyle in which action is woven into our daily lives and feels both inspired *and* manageable.

Vision

Your vision statement should be a succinct and ambitious articulation of the change you want to see in the world. It should center the issue you are going to focus on.

Here's mine: A world where everyone is an activist for justice.

Your turn. What is your vision for change?

Mission

Your mission statement should clarify how you are going to contribute to making that vision a reality. It is a statement of the goal of your activist life.

Here's mine: I use artistic mediums to build community and support community members in connecting their values to their actions. I support their progress by providing endless opportunities for them to grow as critical thinkers and change makers.

Your turn. How will you work for your vision?

It is so much easier to find hope when you have clarified your purpose and committed to having a positive impact on the world every day. Take your vision statement and mission statement and make a piece of art that captures their spirit. Display it in a high-visibility spot in your home. Let it serve as a daily reminder. Let it drive and change you.

The Strategic Activist Lifestyle

It is easy to inspire fear and hate. Frankly, it's lazy. Changing hearts and minds, inspiring empathy, centering community care and mutual aid— that is where the real work lies. It's the work of self-reflection, self- and co-regulation, listening, facing uncomfortable truths, deprogramming, sacrifice, and conflict. It's all the things power holders would prefer we ignore and avoid in service to the status quo. Those who benefit from exploitative and oppressive systems want to keep us in a harmful cycle of outrage, rage, reaction, overwhelm, new outrage, new rage, new reaction, exacerbated overwhelm—all of which ultimately lead to burnout and feelings of hopelessness. The strategy is simply to grind us down: Target a new thing every day through some grandiose and horrific move against humanity. Make us look left, look right, look up, look down, until we are too exhausted to move forward. It's brilliant, really. They weaponize our humanity against us. The body and psyche can take only so much before they concede.

By reframing our approach to the work of equity and justice, we can outmaneuver them. Adopting a lifelong commitment to making impactful change on an issue that provokes us builds resilience and tolerance. Sustained, consistent effort is the winning strategy. We must play the long game—the very long game.

It starts with an understanding of self, a confidence in knowing what we believe and a willingness to close the gap between these beliefs and our actions. Then it must expand outward. Change requires the collective. We need each other. Together, we apply a strategic process, building the path toward our vision, finding joy at every turn through exponential impact. The work moves from reactive and draining to proactive and generative. It's a simple paradigm shift that yields colossal results. Once you turn it on, the activist mindset seeps into every part of your life. You no longer tolerate the injustices you experience or witness in the classroom, boardroom, hospital, party, restaurant, subway, or family holiday. You don't let things slide. You don't make excuses or wave away the comments or slights. You become a full-time, unapologetic activist, and it is fucking powerful.

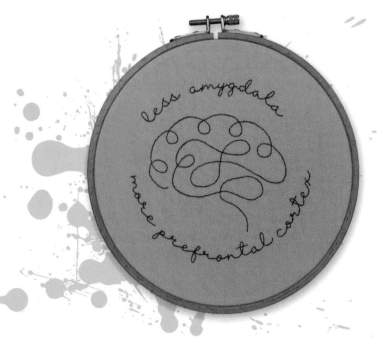

Bumps in the Road

Building a life of balanced activism does not mean it's all smooth sailing. Complicated moments are inevitable, but we can prepare for them and learn from them. We are constantly evolving beings driven by curiosity. The more we learn, the more our ideas grow and change. It is our responsibility to take in new information and assess the changes we need to make to accommodate our shifting understanding of the world— especially when our new understandings lead to revisions in our values.

I am endlessly frustrated with capitalism. It took me decades to understand that many of my frustrations were directly linked to that system. That my feelings of failure and my scarcity mindset were learned and reinforced through societal conditioning. I am still on that journey of realization. How can one live in a capitalist society and be anticapitalist? Hell if I know. I could go live in the woods, off the grid, foraging and crafting to get my basic needs met. But let's be real, I love electricity, plumbing, grocery stores, and my cell phone. There are levels to resisting problematic systems, and I am not willing to shit in the woods for the rest of my life to challenge capitalism. So what *am* I willing to do? This is the question I ask myself a dozen times a day in relation to every choice I make.

I think about every dollar I spend and what those decisions say about my values. Sometimes they say that I choose ease over virtue. I have sculpted a life that offers me freedom over security. I've gone years without health insurance because I didn't want a job that exploited my labor in service to someone else's bottom line. I am strategic about how to make my offerings accessible to as many people as possible while also ensuring I can pay my bills. I live according to my own definitions of success, which don't prioritize accumulating material goods. I like to believe I live on the fringes of capitalism, or at least I am thoughtful in how I interact with the system. Through modeling and sharing my thoughts with others, perhaps I'm helping chip away at it.

Does that feel like enough? No. Is that a conflict that arises in me regularly? Sure is. These internal conflicts help us find a way to do a little better every time they rear up. They teach us. The trick is to face the reality of what they are here to teach us versus allowing them to debilitate us.

IMPERFECT
but trying

ART CHALLENGE!

Create a piece of art that illustrates an internal conflict you possess. Use your making time to help process the tensions you experience and what actions you might take to create more alignment.

Know Your Limits

Our internal conflicts can be a breeze compared to the external conflicts that arise when you live a life of conviction. Everyone will challenge you when you dare to speak your truth. Navigating these conflicts can be the most difficult and consuming part of being an activist. It requires grace, patience, and a seemingly superhuman level of restraint. I like to remind myself that conflicts are practice for creating the world I want to see. I also forgive myself when it all goes terribly wrong with the reminder that I'm doing the best I can, and I'll try again tomorrow.

For myself, sleep is a fantastic predictor of how successful I will be at handling conflict. If I am rested, I can de-escalate a situation with speed and dexterity. If I am tired, I just might flip a table and set it on fire to make my point. Therefore, sleep is a top priority for me. On days when I'm feeling exhausted, I try not put myself in situations where arson might seem like a logical solution. That includes social media. My most cringe-worthy social media moments have always been a result of being tired and reacting to someone or something that triggered my rage.

Any sensation or change in your behavior has something to tell you. Knowing what your body and spirit need to bring your best self to any situation is invaluable as an activist. Do any of the following feel familiar?

- Feeling impatient
- Headaches or body aches
- Lack of sleep
- Trouble getting out of bed
- Watching a lot of television
- Endlessly scrolling through social media
- Overeating or, conversely, lack of appetite
- Consuming more caffeine or alcohol than usual
- Skipping workouts or, conversely, excessively working out
- Taking more or different drugs than normal
- Trouble staying focused or organized
- Lack of creativity
- Loss of motivation
- Crying more than usual

Sometimes you suffer a defeat or setback and need to recover and restrategize. Other times the rest of your life is in flux, and you need to make choices to prioritize your time. Whatever the cause, listening to and respecting the inner cues that signal overwhelm will help prevent burnout.

What are your cues that signal overwhelm? How can you recognize that you need to make a change? Write them down. What do these cues signal to you? What do they want you to do?

WELL, WELL, WELL, IF IT ISN'T THE CONSEQUENCES OF MY OWN ACTIONS

Know It, Say It, Get It: Boundaries

Understanding your limits enables you to know when you need to reset your boundaries. Being a strong self-advocate will ensure those boundaries are heard and respected. Self-advocacy is simply your ability to communicate your needs and negotiate getting those needs met. Simple, but not easy. It takes a keen understanding of self to be able to name your needs. It takes an understanding of others, skills, and strength to get those needs met.

Advocating for yourself can be particularly challenging for change makers, as self-sacrifice is a generally accepted work model. I recently heard a mother talking about her three adult children and their chosen professions. She went on about two of her children who had wonderfully successful *careers* in business. She spoke of their lavish lifestyles and vacations. When she spoke of her third child, she talked about her *vocation*, which had led her to work in the nonprofit sector. She went

on about how this child had no money and worked all the time, but it made her happy because it's more than a job, it is a calling. This expectation of change makers is insidious in our culture. Self-sacrifice is not a vocation. It is a tragedy inflicted on us by the systems of oppression that dominate our culture (and the thinking of the masses).

Everyone needs to advocate for themselves in all areas of their lives. We all deserve to have the support we need. On a personal scale, that can look like conversations with your partner(s) when you feel like the workload in your home is out of balance. It might be a chat with a friend about not having the capacity to talk through their divorce trauma in that moment. Maybe you need to talk to a professor or boss about your workload and negotiate deadlines. On a collective scale, it could look like forming a union, going on strike, or working to change policy on a local or national level.

Self-advocacy is about understanding your rights and your responsibilities. It's about problem solving, speaking up for yourself, and reaching out to others for support. It's about your autonomy and sovereignty.

There are times when the work demands more of you. There are moments when your boundaries are tested. Thanks to the work you put into your strategic planning process, however, you know what to do. You circle back to your goals and your resource map. You adjust them.

ART CHALLENGE!

Create a piece of work that reminds you of the things you do when you need to reconnect with your power and your peace. Spend some sacred time loving on yourself in this way. Let it remind you of the ways in which you care for yourself. Let it inspire you to be your own advocate.

relentlessly advocate
for yourself

You reallocate resources or focus on acquiring the new resources you need to meet the moment. You adjust your goals, if need be. Self-sacrifice is not the answer for you or your team. Movements implode when we abandon our physical and emotional needs. This is why our strategy is so important. It protects us all; it keeps our movements strong and moving forward. Oppressors count on us failing from exhaustion and lack of resources. We outperform through strategy.

Self-advocacy is not just about setting boundaries when things get hectic. It's about proactively creating spaces and ways of working that build in play, celebration, rest, and processing time. It's inventing a new way of doing the work and collaborating that rejects the dominant systems and reimagines what is possible. The process presented in this book offers you plenty of opportunity to incorporate these moments into your plans. You work through them as a team early on. You add them to your goals, timelines, and calendars. They serve as markers of success. They are nonnegotiables. You find your power and your peace in these steps. You honor the work that you are doing and have done. There you will find the strength and enthusiasm to joyfully carry on.

Calling In Crew

As we have talked about, there are plenty of moments that require us to lean on our community. The beauty of a collaborative activist network is that we can show up to lend support or provide relief to other movements at pivotal moments. While we are all working on our own chosen issues within movements, all issues are connected, and there are times when we must rally in support of our comrades in justice.

When Donald Trump enacted an executive action that restricted travel to the United States from seven majority-Muslim countries, I made a sign, met up with my squad, and headed straight to O'Hare airport to join in the emergency protest at the international terminal. The protest was initiated by the Arab American Action Network and was supported by several leading organizations and elected officials in Chicago. The activists who organized the protest were the local experts and leaders on the issues facing Muslim and Asian Americans in Chicago and Illinois. Community showed up when asked. We listened. We learned more about the demands of the community and what additional support they needed in the moment.

Emergency immigration protest at
O'Hare airport in Chicago, 2017

Years later, with the precipitous rise in xenophobic violence brought about by the language of power holders regarding the pandemic, I partnered with some of these organizations. I invited my community to join us in bystander intervention trainings led by these activists. I offered my art in exchange for donations to their work. I was able to use my social capital and resources in allyship with targeted communities. More importantly, my community showed up and trained up on how they can intervene when they witness harassment or violence in public. Together, we expanded the reach.

These were both obvious all-hands-on-deck moments. It's not always the case that we can see when change makers are overwhelmed, which is why it's important to ask for help when we need it. When we know we're needed, we bring our knowledge and resources to support the work being done by the experts. We offer up what we have.

Collaboration in a Society of Rugged Individualism

Learning how to work in communion with others is a radical act in a society build on individualism, sustained by capitalism, and currently steeped in social media—induced self-focus. Competition is the lens through which dominant culture gauges success. Activist communities are not immune to this conditioning. But competition is toxic. One of my former clients was a national nonprofit that worked to fund research for a debilitating disease. We were discussing why they wanted to improve their messaging and tactics. The executive director stated that a celebrity who was living with the disease had started a competing nonprofit that was getting all the attention and exponentially more funding. They needed to compete harder.

This is not unusual, especially within institutions that rely on philanthropic and government funding to do their work. This horizontal

interdependence is the answer

hostility, or competition among seeming allies, can be seen at all levels of activism, from interpersonal to institutional.

For some, simply being in a room where folks speak freely and are met with respect is revolutionary. Much of the work of activism can be found right here in the construction of communities that model what we want for the world at large. When we learn how to shed ego and control in service to the change that we are working to create, we find true belonging.

This is why I lean on art. Art creates opportunities for people to enjoy the experience of trying to work together. Art keeps the pressure low and offers an on-ramp to the more challenging community work that comes with sustained activist efforts. We don't teach children the alphabet and then hand them a book to read. There are critical steps in between. The same goes for collaboration and activism.

As we have explored throughout this book, a spirit of collaboration is intentional. It demands that we examine conflict and engage in radical honesty. It is a constant negotiation with seasons of peace and tension. With the entrance or exit of any member comes a reorientation period.

Group dynamics are constantly shifting. Therefore, constant communication is vital.

A major challenge that exists in creating truly collaborative spaces is when we butt up against ego—our own and that of others. Nothing is sustainable alone, and yet it's rare to be working in community with one another and exist ego-free. This is why our strategic process is so important. A clearly articulated shared purpose is a powerful tool in combating ego. Return to your shared vision in moments of tension. Together, you have been crafting your goals, messaging, and tactics. You have found compromise and identified your path to success. You have explored the pathways to the vision and agreed on the route. The steps in the process are the building blocks of successful collaboration.

I once attempted to bring together a group that I thought would be a fantastic team to work through a craftivism intervention. It was clear early on that this collection of people had wildly different comfort levels with how radical they were willing to go when approaching a project. After a few meetings, I knew it was not going to work. We would require so much compromise from everyone, across the board, that no one was going to feel satisfied. So we lovingly disbanded (Goop joke). In other words, it's okay to say, "This just isn't going to work." You can believe in the same thing but disagree on how to get there. There's nothing wrong with agreeing to take different paths.

What's at Stake

White supremacist ideology, patriarchy, and capitalism dominate our lives in ways that range from obvious to insidious. These systems of oppression create the dominant power structures that we live under. I know this is not news to you. It is important to remember that activists come to the work with vastly different things at stake. For some, activism might challenge our comfort zones or stress relationships. For others, activism is a mechanism of survival. We need to understand our positioning relative to power in all aspects of our lives in order to be

YOUR TOLERANCE
FOR RISK
GROWS ALONGSIDE
YOUR OUTRAGE

effective change makers. Our privileges should motivate us. The places where we hold power offer us opportunity to leverage it for change.

When I hear craftivism described as a humbler, gentler, quieter form of protest, I hear judgment and privilege. When I see craftivism being uplifted as an alternative to megaphones and marches, I see judgment and privilege. We all have different tolerance levels when it comes to resistance. (As I noted earlier, I draw the line at shitting in the woods to resist capitalism.) That said, when we start gatekeeping and policing what is and isn't an acceptable form of resistance for others, we are harming our own movements.

Knowing your boundaries and limits is important and valid. Imposing them on others is violence. Comfort zones can be set by privilege but also by fear. Comfort zones are not static. As you grow your comfort zones or they are forced to expand, you will find that things you never dreamed of doing now sound like great ideas. So many people who had never before been to a protest made a sign and headed to the Women's March in 2017. Their outrage at what they had seen moved them to new action. These same people have engaged in myriad activist activities since then. Fear and rage expanded their risk tolerance.

We've seen young people enter capitol buildings en masse and demand that politicians do something about gun violence. We've seen community members who feel disempowered, unseen, and under-resourced break windows and destroy property. We've seen people beaten, gassed, and arrested for standing up for their beliefs. We've seen people self-immolate to protest war.

When things change, our tolerance level for risk and sacrifice will change. There is no one right way of doing things. What works for us might not work for others and vice versa. These are moments of tension that invite us to explore our privileges, fears, and judgments. They should not become opportunities to create horizontal hostilities. We all have unique human experiences that shape our view and experience of the world. If we disagree with someone's approach, we can focus our energy on creating a world where they won't feel like they have to take those actions.

That's that, then.

Activism is a lifelong commitment to creating the kind of world you want to live in. An activist lifestyle means holding the vision while keeping perspective. It requires a plan, commitment, community, and an understanding of your resources and boundaries.

An activist mindset is framed by curiosity, inquiry, and critical thought. It drives you to dig deeper and see with increasing clarity the negative impacts that systems of oppression have on every aspect of your life and world. Then it demands you take action.

Narrowing your focus and committing to a cause frees you from the overwhelming cycle of rage and reaction that can come when confronting harsh realities. It allows you to develop strategies and become an expert in service to impact. It ensures sustained action and grows resilience. When this commitment is rooted in self-knowing and supported through community, your efforts can be generative and joyful. When the work is fulfilling and your boundaries are firm, you avoid burnout. Your schedule allows for rest and recovery because you have built it in. You have created an approach to the work that won't force you to retreat from it. There is nothing more harmful to the spirit of a movement than waves of allyship and support that recede when things get intense.

Change making demands that you learn and grow from your fears instead of leaping to judgment. It expands awareness of your privileges and motivates you to leverage them with the goal of relinquishing them. Through the process, you learn to be an advocate not just for others but for yourself. It takes patience, empathy, and understanding. It asks you to bring your best self to the table every time—and that's no small feat.

The power of art lies in shaping culture, engaging community, and finding voice. Using these tools to expand the work of activist movements is transformative. Centering and supporting activism with art is a powerful way to proliferate the impact of your work. Art offers a portal to collaboration and community and a mechanism for advocacy. Creativity is the single most valuable asset in reimagining what is possible. There is no transformation without art. There is no transformation without you.

Group hug!

PLANNING TEMPLATES
TIME TO MOVE THE NEEDLE

Life as an activist calls for self-awareness, a commitment to consistent work on a cause you are passionate about, and a strategic plan to guide the work. Throughout this book, you have engaged in activities, considered different perspectives, and dug deep to home in on the issue you want to commit a lifetime to working on. You've learned a strategic process that can direct and support your efforts. In our final chapter together, I offer you a workspace where you can synthesize the outcomes of your efforts as well as a planning space for your future accomplishments.

I AM AN ACTIVIST

THE WORLD I WANT TO LIVE IN

Describe the kind of world you want to live in. What does it look, feel, and sound like? Articulate your vision for a future in which humanity achieves peace and justice. Turn this vision into a piece of art. Let the process expand the depth of your ideals and values.

In Chapter 10, you clarified your vision and mission statements—your purpose and path. Write them here.

VISION STATEMENT
Your vision statement should be a succinct and ambitious articulation of the change you want to see in the world. It should center the issue you are going to focus on.

_____

_____

_____

_____

MISSION STATEMENT
Your mission statement should make clear how you will contribute to your vision.

_____

_____

_____

_____

YOUR SINGULAR ISSUE
What cause have you decided to focus the majority of your activist efforts on with your remaining years?

_____

_____

OWN IT

In Chapter 3, we looked at some of the activist roles that exist in the social change ecosystem. Activism can look different for everyone. What are some of the skills and talents you could employ as an activist? It's time to flex, my friend. List them all! Own your badassery.

_____

_____

_____

_____

RESEARCH

Consuming and listening are important steps in enhancing understanding of your cause. Going deep down the rabbit hole will enrich your knowledge of the nuances and complexities of the issues. Awareness of counterarguments and perspectives is valuable information as well. Take notice of those you diverge from or disagree with.

Who are you reading, following, and listening to? Where are you getting your information from? What are some topline takeaways? What are you learning?

_____

_____

_____

_____

_____

_____

I TAKE ACTION

Now that you have done the personal development work, it's time to start building your plan. Throughout the book, we used the case study of a community beach cleanup to illustrate the various steps in the process. We'll use that same example to model how to use this planning template. This process can be used to create projects and action plans for any scale of work, from an individual action to a global movement. Don't you just love a strategic process?!

IDENTIFYING PROBLEMS

Using your lived experiences, observations, and research, identify the problems you as a change maker see and seek to address. Consider the potential human, environmental, physical, organizational, and systemic impacts.

> Case Study: There are a growing number of used hypodermic needles on the beaches in Weymouth, Massachusetts.

_____

_____

_____

_____

_____

_____

IDENTIFYING ROOT CAUSES

Drill down on each problem you have found until you can identify and articulate some of the root causes of these problems using the *Why?* method.

> Case Study:
>
> *Why?* People who use drugs get high on the beach and then discard their used needles there.
>
> *Why?* It's a mostly deserted spot at night, and they can get high out of sight.
>
> *Why?* It's illegal to use recreational drugs, and they could get arrested and put in jail if they are caught.
>
> *Why?* The United States has a mostly punitive system in place to punish people who use drugs.
>
> *Why?* There is a pervasive misunderstanding of how and why people use drugs, and instead of working to understand and support their recovery, we criminalize their actions.

Why?

Why?

Why?

Why?

Why?

THE TEAM

First things first: Are you joining or building a team?

If you are interested in *joining* a team, think through the type of group you would like to be a part of, what you can bring to the table, and what you hope to get out of the experience.

- Who do you want to work with? Describe the spirit, intention, approach, and goals of your dream team.
- What role do you want to serve?
- How do you see yourself working with the team?
- What skill sets and talents can you bring to the group?
- Review your flex list and decide which talents would best apply, given the role you hope to serve.
- What do you want to get out of the experience? What you want matters, too!

If you are *building* a team, think through the type of group you need to craft to make change.

> Case Study: We are building a team of motivated neighbors who care about the safety of our local beaches and the care and safety of all our community members, including those who use drugs. It would be helpful if initial team members were connected to other community members, local leaders, harm reduction professionals, politicians, business leaders, and officials. Helpful skills would include fundraising, marketing, event planning, and graphic design.

- Who would care about the issue you are focusing on?
- What is the intention, spirit, and energy you want this group to embody?
- Whose voices should be heard and included?
- What skill sets do you know you need in this group?
- What talents do you think you might need in this group?
- Is the group open to everyone, or is it restricted?

BRAINSTORMING

Now that you have a refined understanding of the problem, you can begin to brainstorm solutions. There are no bad ideas. Remember your vision. List out all the ways (micro to macro) in which you would want to address the problem.

> Case Study: Potential solutions include beach cleanup, sharps containers on the beach, making naloxone and testing strips available on the beach, mobile needle exchange program, awareness campaign, education campaign, safe consumption site, more resources to support people with substance use disorders, mutual aid group, and policy changes.

RESOURCE MAP

Resource mapping is a twofold process. First identify your personal resources. Then clarify the team resources. This helps you determine which actions from your brainstorm you can feasibly start with. It protects your boundaries and allows you to scale the work.

> Case Study:
>
> *My Resources*
> - 10 hours a month for two months
> - $50
> - Loads of enthusiasm and motivation
> - Friend relationship with 3 neighbors
>
> *Group Resources (on Day 1)*
> - 4 volunteers
> - 35 hours a month for two months
> - $100
> - 15 close neighbor connections
> - Experience with fundraising, event planning, and graphic design

List your available resources: time, money, network, et cetera.

List the collective resources of the team.

POWER MAP

Your power map creates a visual understanding of the relational landscape of your issue to help you find collaborators. It's an assessment of who holds power, their beliefs on your issue, and how your team connects to them.

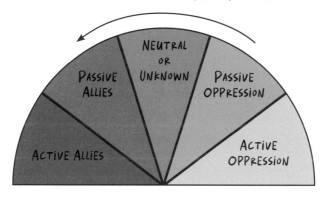

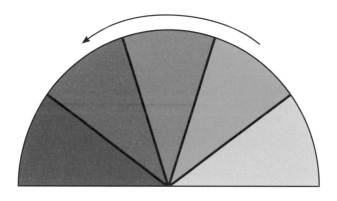

Review your brainstorm, resource map, and power map. Determine a
realistic first action.

> Case Study: Based on our resource and power maps, the team has
> determined that a beach cleanup is a manageable first action.

_____

_____

S.S.M.A.R.T.E.R. GOALS

It is time to set some goals! As a reminder, S.S.M.A.R.T.E.R. stands for
sentiment-led, specific, measurable, attainable, relevant, time-bound,
evaluated, and readjusted. What do you want to accomplish?

> Case Study:
> - By June 2, we will have recruited a 10-person team to plan and
>   organize the beach cleanup.
> - By June 16, the team will have created a volunteer plan, a supply
>   list, and a schedule for the day of the cleanup.
> - By June 30, we will have at least 25 volunteers registered and
>   assigned roles for the beach cleanup.
> - By July 3, we will have purchased or gathered all materials and
>   stored them in Shannon's garage.
> - On July 5, at least 35 volunteers will assemble at Shannon's house,
>   gather supplies, and participate in the beach cleanup.
> - On July 6, Shannon will bake cookies and deliver them to everyone
>   who participated in the beach cleanup.

Goal 1: _____

_____

Goal 2: _____

_____

Goal 3:

Goal 4:

Goal 5:

POTENTIAL BARRIERS

Your goals help you identify potential barriers. Review your goals and jot down any issues you can see.

Case Study:

- Our cranky neighbor might object to the event.
- Safety concerns over handling and disposing of used needles might limit who joins in.
- We might need a permit to block off a portion of the street for safety and accessibility.

AUDIENCE AND MESSAGING

A vital step in the strategic process is the development of messaging that speaks to and moves your audience to action.

- Who do you want to connect with?
- What do you want the messaging to accomplish?
- How do you want your audience to feel?
- What do you want them to do?
- What is already being said?
- What is missing?
- Is your messaging hashtag and social media friendly?

> Case Study:
>
> *Audience:* Neighbors living within a five-block radius of the beach
>
> *Message:* This Community Cares

Describe your target audience:

_____

_____

_____

_____

_____

_____

Compose your primary messages:

_____

_____

_____

_____

_____

TACTICS

Now is your moment to clarify all the actions you will take to meet your goals and spread your message. Developing strategic tactics for change making requires a combination of ingenuity, marketing, advertising, and execution. This is where you really get crafty and creative. Go wild!

Case Study:

Digital Tactics

- Facebook event
- Post in neighborhood Facebook group and relevant interest groups

Analog Tactics

- Posters throughout the neighborhood
- Craft night
- Educational zine invitation on every doorstep
- Live music at the event
- Collaborative art mosaic using beach trash
- This Community Cares buttons
- Chalking
- Harm reduction specialists tabling at event
- Naloxone and testing strip distribution

Digital Tactics:

_____

_____

_____

Analog Tactics:

_____

_____

_____

_____

ACCESSIBILITY AND RESPONSIBILITY

Evaluate your tactics and process for environmental and social responsibility.

Case Study:

- Cleanup will take place on a weekend.
- Zines and posters will have accessible design.
- Live music performance times will be clearly articulated.
- Vegan, nut-free, and gluten-free snacks will be provided.
- A beach wheelchair will be available through the parks department.
- All interactive components will take place on the street for folks who aren't able to access the beachfront.
- Mosaic art will upcycle safe beach trash.
- We'll borrow a button maker from the library.
- We'll use supplies from the Creative Reuse space.
- Single-use plastic bags will be upcycled into plarn and macraméd into bags for participants.
- Flyers will be put up using nontoxic wheatpaste.

Environmental considerations: Consider how to reduce, reuse, upcycle, and recycle.

_____

_____

Accessibility plans: Revisit the list in Chapter 8 to get you started.

_____

_____

Sourcing plans: How will you prioritize local, independent, BIPOC-owned, women-owned, queer-owned, or other categories of resources?

_____

_____

DOCUMENTATION

Create a list of all the documents you will need to manage your team and initiatives, including timelines, calendars, budget and finance management systems, contact management systems, photo and video folders, evaluations, and assessment tools.

Case Study:

- Timeline
- Group calendar
- Budget
- Volunteer contacts
- Shared drive for notes, pics, and videos

_____

_____

_____

_____

CELEBRATIONS

Planning your celebrations is part of the strategic process. This is how you honor what you have accomplished, mark progress, and keep momentum. Come up with a list of ways you will commemorate your wins!

Case Study:

- Homemade pizza at kickoff meeting
- Buttons for volunteers
- Slideshow, superlative awards, and loads of cookies at wrap-up meeting

_____

_____

_____

_____

ASSESSMENT

When you have completed the action or project, you should assess how it went. Did you meet your goals? Why or why not? What were the highlights of the experience? What were the lowlights? What did you learn? What do you want to remember or change for next time? What sort of feedback did you receive?

Case Study:

- 12 volunteers were on the planning committee by May 20.
- 43 volunteers/attendees were at the beach cleanup.
- The city granted us a permit to block off part of the street.
- 6 trash bags of waste were removed from the beach.
- Community clinic representatives attended and distributed information, naloxone, and testing strips.
- We made a rad mosaic with the safe waste.
- We ran out of snacks halfway through.
- Several neighbors ran back to their houses for folding chairs for community elders.
- One kiddo fell and scraped up their knee, and we didn't have a first-aid kit on hand.
- The music kept things lively, but our cranky neighbor called the police to complain.
- Police made us turn down the music.
- The event was spirited and positive.
- Some problematic language was used (and corrected by the harm reduction team).
- A number of people asked when we were going to do it again.

_____

_____

_____

_____

_____

WHAT IS NEXT?

After a celebration and a rest, it's time to make your next plan. Will you iterate, pivot, escalate, or call it a day? Drop your next move here, and then start the process all over again.

> Case Study: We are ready to escalate. We will launch an educational campaign on International Overdose Awareness Day. Strategic planning process, here we come!

_____

_____

_____

_____

_____

It is my greatest hope that you find this helpful.
I look forward to seeing all that you bring forth as we work
toward a more just, healthy, and loving world.

Here's an embroidery pattern just for you. Stitch it, hang it, live it.

Satin Stitch
4 strands

Stem Stitch
3 strands

Whipped Back Stitch
6 strands

ACKNOWLEDGMENTS

When my Uncle Paul learned of my book, he was quick to tell me to keep my acknowledgments short and sweet. "Don't make it a big story. Just thank the people you need to thank."

So picture it . . . Sicily, 1945.

Just kidding! Here is me getting to the point and thanking who I need to thank.

First and foremost, I bow down to my agent, Myrsini Stephanides. This adventure would not and could not have happened without her. She is a total badass and has made this journey as stress-free and fun as anyone could. I admire the shit out of her.

My deepest thanks to the incredible team at Storey Publishing who went above and beyond and did so at a pace that would make The Flash jealous. You got me, saw the vision, and made it happen. Epic.

Huge gratitude and big hugs to Viveka Ray-Mazumder, Steven Moon, and Jill Garvey for the time they put into helping me ensure my case studies were comprehensive and accurate beyond what my own memory could hold.

Love and respect to my parents, Paula and Martin, who instilled in me a deep understanding of self-advocacy, righteousness, and community organizing. They modeled creativity and celebration as a core component to activism and change making. And to my grandmother, Elizabeth McGovern, who worked as a Lowell mill girl her entire life. I'm certain textiles are in my bones because of her.

Shout-out to my brother, Brian, who is an incredible artist. I grow prouder of him every day. Keep doing what you are doing, sir.

Profound love and gratitude for my squad and brain trust who keep me fed, watered, walked, sane, and in check. I am your biggest fan. April McKibban, Brian Assmus, David Baum, Diane Knoepke, Dushaun Branch Pollard, Erin Claudio, Greta Johnsen, Jennifer Sutherland, Jill Garvey, John Marovich, Laura Grimes, Mac Webster, Mark Germain, Mary Morten, Melissa White, Mindy Tsonas Choi, Omkari Williams, the Hackford-Peers, Tuyet Le, and Zayre Ferrer.

I need to immortalize my gratitude to my friends Rebecca Loebe and Chris Loebe, who literally saved my life during the great freeze in Austin, Texas. I love you.

May we never forget the two greatest dogs that ever walked this earth, Maggie and Scrappy. I miss them every single day, and they were napping on my feet when I started writing this book.

Thank you to Mrs. Kathy Puleo, who taught me how to cross-stitch. To my aunt Hellen Drown, who taught me to sew and made me the greatest Halloween costumes that Weymouth, Massachusetts, has ever seen.

I would be aimless if it weren't for the communities I am a part of that keep me inspired, motivated, and empowered to stay in the fight. Thank you, Seriously Badass Women, Sew Culty (not an actual cult . . . but I guess that is what someone in a cult would say), the Rita's Quilt crew, Dan Ward and my workout buddies, my Patreon community, and my forever family from UMass #BCGForever.

Thank YOU, reader, for your support, energy, and attention. I can't wait to see what you do next!

INDEX

Page numbers in *italics* indicate photos or illustrations.